What can I do with...
a social sciences degree?

Beryl Dixon

TROTMAN

What can I do with… a social sciences degree?
This first edition published in 2003 by Trotman and Company Ltd
2 The Green, Richmond, Surrey TW9 1PL

Statistics from *What do graduates do?* are quoted with kind
permission from AGCAS.

The HESA data quoted in this publication is from the HESA Student
Record July 2001; © Higher Education Statistics Agency Limited 2002.

The Higher Education Statistics Agency (HESA) does not accept any
responsibility for any references or conclusions derived from the
data quoted in this publication.

British Library Cataloguing in Publication Data
A catalogue record for this book is available from the British Library

ISBN 0 85660 867 X

Typeset by Mac Style Ltd, Scarborough, N. Yorkshire

Printed and bound in Great Britain by Creative Print and Design
(Wales) Ltd

Contents

About the author

Beryl Dixon is an experienced careers adviser who has worked in different careers companies and in tertiary college, where she advised students of all ages on employment and higher education choices. She has also worked for the Ministry of Defence and the Department for Education and Skills, visiting schools in Hong Kong, Cyprus, Brussels and Luxembourg to provide careers advice to the children of expatriate service personnel and government officials.

She now concentrates on careers writing and is the author of several books on careers and higher education. She also writes for a number of careers publications, including *Youcan*, UCAS' magazine for A-level students, and for national newspapers including *The Times* and the *Independent*. Her other titles published by Trotman are *Getting into Art & Design, Getting into Hotels and Catering* and *What can I do with… an arts degree?*

She is herself a modern languages graduate.

Acknowledgements

I would like to thank Martin Pennington of Leicester University Careers Advisory Service, and Keith Thompson of Reading University Careers Advisory Service for their help when I was researching this book. Thanks also Martin Pennington and to Christina Cherry at the University of Greenwich Press Office and Stephen Laing at the University of Teesside Press Office, for their help in tracking down graduates prepared to be interviewed for the book.

Introduction

The government has set a target of 50 per cent of the 18-plus age group experiencing higher education. Forty per cent already do so – but no one yet knows what effect the recent decision to allow universities and colleges to charge top-up tuition fees might have.

There is no doubt that higher education costs money – even at today's fee rates. Does it bring benefits? Why should young people think it worthwhile to make such a major investment?

The most obvious benefit is financial. In 2002 researchers at the London School of Economics investigated the effect of different qualifications on an individual's earnings. They estimated that whereas the possession of two or more A-levels increased earnings by 16 per cent, a first degree is estimated to produce an increase of around 26 per cent. For men, having a degree raises salaries by 29 per cent in the private sector and by 17 per cent in the public sector. For women the figures were 30 per cent and 25 per cent.

The average starting salary for 2002 graduates was £18,700 – and could be over £20,000 in 2003 if they rise by an expected 2.5 per cent. (The second figure comes from a report commissioned by the Association of Graduate Recruiters, an organisation of employers that recruit graduates every year.)

Research carried out by higher education careers services concludes that between the ages of 21 and 30, graduates' earnings increase by 50.1 per cent compared with only 28.7 per cent for people without a degree.

Can these levels be sustained with ever increasing numbers going through higher education? You might think not, but according to the LSE study the rates of return have hardly varied in the period it has been conducting studies (1993 to 2002). The study concluded that demand for higher qualifications is constantly rising; consequently we have not yet reached the point where too many people are entering higher education.

A second benefit should surely be that of finding more rewarding jobs. Do graduates automatically find more interesting jobs than non-graduates? It has to be said that some do enter what might not be thought of as graduate jobs – and often complain when they start work that their abilities and knowledge are not fully used. But quite often it is necessary to gain experience in a lower level job before being fully stretched. Research by the University of Warwick shows that less than 10 per cent of graduates were still in 'non-graduate' jobs three and a half years after graduation, and at that point only 2 per cent of those available for work were unemployed.

Do only people who have done vocational degrees and have technical skills get well-paid jobs? No. A third benefit of higher education is that students gain some valuable *soft* or *transferable* skills that are valued by employers. University or college life gives students several opportunities to gain such skills: joining societies and gaining work experience are two of them. Even the fact that most students have to have part-time jobs to eke out their finances is a blessing in disguise. You can acquire a lot of skills and experience in even mundane jobs! With so many graduates chasing the most interesting jobs you will need as much as possible on your CV to be able to compete. *A degree alone is no guarantee of a job.*

This book looks at skills and qualifications most required by employers and the activities that students can use to 'add value' to their CVs. There are points made by employers. There are also chapters on five different social science courses, showing any general trends in employment from students of those subjects.

Why these subjects? Because 'social science' is very difficult to define. Some universities include culture, media and communication studies under this heading. Others include accountancy, business studies, religious studies and philosophy. There are lots of courses with titles like community studies, development studies, gender studies, international relations, public administration and social policy. The most common subjects however are economics, geography, law, politics, psychology and sociology (which includes related subjects like anthropology and criminology). Law is not included here because it is the subject of a separate book, *What can I do with... a law degree?* Nor is philosophy, which is covered in a chapter in *What can I do with... an arts degree?* But please do not think that certain careers automatically follow certain subjects. What can be done by a politics graduate can usually be done equally well by someone with a degree in sociology or geography.

When researching the book I contacted a number of universities asking if it was possible to put me in touch with graduates from five subject areas who were willing to describe their jobs and explain how their degree courses had helped them to get them. You can read about the experiences of some of them in Chapters 3–7. The response from some universities was so enthusiastic that I had to decline some offers and I had to miss out:

★ economics graduates working as accountants, building society managers and independent financial advisers
★ a human geography graduate working as a market researcher
★ a psychology graduate working as an assistant psychologist with people who have learning disabilities
★ a politics graduate working as a personnel manager
★ a sociology graduate working for the National Youth Agency.

1 Myths and facts

Just what will you be able to do with a social science degree? You cannot, obviously, become an architect, dentist, physicist, rocket scientist – or a host of other things for which vocational degrees are required. But that still leaves a large number of jobs!

Many students who have done a social science degree want to make direct use of it in a career. There are possibilities to do this, which are listed in each of the subject chapters. You should note now, however, that many of these careers will require you to do further training. To become a social worker, chartered psychologist or surveyor, for instance, it is necessary to train and study for professional qualifications, while a Master's degree is often advantageous for anyone hoping to work as a professional economist. Each chapter also gives a list of 'next best' options – a number of careers in which the subject is particularly relevant.

By doing a social science degree you will acquire several common skills (regardless of whether you do economics, geography or psychology). You will study some subjects within your degree course that will require you to handle data and figures, some that involve conducting surveys, experiments or fieldwork, which will give you skills in working in a team, others for which you will have to read widely and write essays. You will also learn to give presentations and take part in discussions. You will be able to:

★ analyse, interpret and evaluate information
★ respect cultural differences (very important since many employers now recruit globally)
★ communicate verbally

★ communicate in writing
★ make decisions
★ manage projects (through managing your own time and workload)
★ solve problems
★ use IT
★ use research methods
★ work with other people.

You will also have an insight into human behaviour. This will be valuable in whatever career you ultimately choose. Two people who feature as case studies in this book mention this in particular (see Claire Paczko, page 85, and Tim Guymer, page 57).

But that's not all! You will also be able to choose careers that are open to graduates in any discipline. Around 55 per cent of jobs advertised for graduates do not require a particular subject. Some of these are mentioned in each subject chapter. If you look at another book in this series, *What can I do with… an arts degree?*, you will find a chapter listing almost 80 different careers that come into this category. Ones that do not feature in this book as case studies include: administrator, advertising (account executive or copywriter), air traffic controller, antique dealer, archivist, arts administrator, auctioneer and valuer, bank manager, barrister, bookseller, broadcasting (editor, producer, programme assistant or reporter), building society manager, buyer, charity fundraiser, civil servant, company secretary, computer programmer, conference and/or events manager, customs and excise officer, diplomat, estate or lettings agent, freight forwarder, health service manager, hotel manager, housing manager, human resources (personnel) officer, immigration officer, indexer, information manager/scientist, IT consultant, insurance (broker, claims assessor or underwriter), journalist, leisure manager, librarian, local government officer, logistics manager, loss adjuster, management consultant, market research executive, marketing manager, merchant navy officer, museum curator, officer in one of the armed forces, police officer, prison governor, probation officer, public relations executive, publishing (editor, picture researcher or proof reader), purchasing officer, recruitment consultant, retail manager, solicitor, tourism manager, tourist information centre manager, training officer/manager, travel industry manager and web designer.

Not a bad list, is it?

The case studies in each of the chapters in this book have been chosen deliberately to show graduates in careers that do make direct use of their degree subject. But you might want more detail on some of the other possibilities. *What can I do with… an arts degree?* has case studies of graduates working as the following:

★ chartered accountant
★ contracts officer
★ hotel manager
★ human resources manager
★ investment banking analyst
★ librarian/researcher at the House of Commons
★ magazine editor
★ management consultant
★ naval officer
★ pensions administrator
★ police officer
★ production secretary with the BBC
★ retail manager
★ solicitor
★ web consultant.

If you read about them, you will see that your skills will qualify you for these careers too.

If any of the careers that require further qualifications interest you, you can find all the information you need on entry and training routes in a good careers reference book. (For suggested titles see Chapter 8.) You do not always have to do a full-time course (and find the necessary funding). *Some* employers sponsor graduates through relevant courses on a part-time basis.

It's as well to be aware now that study does not always end when you get a degree! Many careers require further study for professional examinations. Would-be accountants, for example, join their employers as trainees (confusingly known as 'students' if they are in chartered accountancy). They are trained by their employers, learn while doing the job, but have to work in their spare time towards professional examinations set by the different accountancy bodies. Only when they pass them do they become fully qualified. You can read about Matt Clifford's experience on page 31. Probation officers, social workers and financial advisers, including stockbrokers, *must* obtain appropriate qualifications in order to practise their professions. In other careers, qualifications exist but are optional. Having said that, many employers will expect graduates to obtain them. Most organisations would want their human resources staff to become qualified through the Chartered Institute of Personnel and Development, for example, or journalists to obtain NCTJ (National Council for the Training of Journalists) qualifications.

Myths

★ Social science degrees are vocational courses
★ Social science students are 'boxed in'. Their degrees do not qualify them for a wide range of careers
★ They all go into social or welfare work.

Facts

★ About 55 per cent of jobs advertised for graduates do not require a specific degree subject
★ Social science graduates have specific skills *plus* a general level of ability and transferable skills valued by employers

What can I do with... a social sciences degree?

★ Many people doing the same jobs have degrees in English, sociology, geography or even maths, biology or engineering
★ Further study is often required to gain professional qualifications.

What are employers looking for? 2

Why do companies employ graduates at all? Is it simply for their in-depth knowledge of a subject? Not always, and certainly less so in the case of social science and arts graduates than where pure and applied scientists are concerned. Of the subjects featured in this book, psychology and economics are *required* for certain careers. They are *useful* in dozens of others, as are the other social science subjects. Why? Because they teach common skills that are useful in employment.

Problem solving and analysis

Social science courses require students to do fieldwork, laboratory work (psychology) or conduct surveys. Before the students can begin they have to make sure that they understand the problem thoroughly, work out what they are being asked to find, create the working method, carry out the task and present the results. In other words, they tackle a problem by working through it logically in order to come up with a solution. In the workplace this skill can translate into developing policy, solving management or financial problems or planning use of resources (including people). Philip Robinson (page 92) spent most of the first three months in his job writing a detailed proposal for his managers on how a project should be set up.

Reasoning

Some topics taught on social science courses require students to write seminar papers or essays. Most courses offer the choice of doing a dissertation in place of one or more examinations. Students have to use the evidence they have found to present a case and argue it conclusively. They may have to read large amounts of material while doing their research. This gives them skills in deciding what is relevant to the work in hand and discarding the remainder. Claire Paczko (page 85) uses this skill constantly when preparing to go to court as an advocate with her clients.

Working with other people

This skill cannot be over-emphasised. You should learn to defend your opinion under pressure in discussion groups. You should also learn to respect other people's opinions and know when to give in! Often in the real world there is no ideal solution, or if there is, it is too expensive and adjustments have to be made. Colin Wood (see page 42), who works as a surveyor, stresses this point and talks about his need to be diplomatic and able to negotiate.

Teamwork is important too. Many people, especially new graduates, work in small teams or groups. The same requirement to respect other people is there – but there may also be a need to share out the work and decide which individual will be responsible for which parts of the task. Might geography fieldwork and conducting social or political surveys have a relevance here?

IT skills

IT skills are taught and used on social science courses. Some social scientists may decide to make a career in computing and information technology. For the majority, though, this will be a skill that can be used in many careers today. Employers now almost take for granted the ability to use computers, IT and the Internet. Politics graduate Barry Griffiths (see page 54) was able to get, first, a useful vacation placement, then a permanent job because he was already IT literate.

Numeracy

An advantage held by social science graduates over students in some subjects is that their courses are almost bound to have included training in research methods and statistics. They should have little difficulty in convincing employers that they are numerate.

Communication skills

The above are the main skills common to social science students. In addition, shared with students on arts courses, you will have the ability to communicate. This is linked to working with people but can also mean producing written material. Experience in discussion groups and workshops helps in giving presentations, whether these are briefings round a table for colleagues, or full-blown presentations to clients. You will doubtless leave university or college competent to give presentations using PowerPoint or similar aids.

Self-management

In common with all graduates, you will learn to take responsibility for your own learning and to manage your time. Essay deadlines, reading lists, projects to complete – several things due on the same date will give you good training in this. Some courses in which there is a small number of timetabled hours but much work to be done in libraries, etc (politics springs to mind), teach self-discipline. In fact most first-year students find that they have much more free time than they had at school. There are all sorts of opportunities to use it unwisely. It may be difficult at first, but eventually most students learn the arts of self-discipline and time management. This transfers to a job as what Danny Thompson (page 39) refers to as the skill of 'juggling several balls at the same time'.

Finally, you will have learnt to cope and solve problems while working under pressure and to a tight deadline. What else have you been doing when taking exams? The exam room is a real test of ability to remain calm and get the brain going.

To beat off the competition for jobs these days though, you need to offer more. You will also need to demonstrate what employers call personal, transferable skills. They are also known as *core* or *key* skills.

Jobs entered by graduates are changing. A smaller proportion now join traditional graduate training schemes. (Some companies put selected graduates through carefully planned training programmes on which they gain experience in several departments.) Around 15,000 in 2003 are likely to be recruited to such programmes. But 150,000 in total are expected to find work in the year after they graduate. Many employers now recruit graduates directly into specific jobs – and expect them to begin to contribute almost immediately. While encouraging and supporting, they will expect graduates to take much more responsibility for their own learning and to request support in areas in which they feel less competent, or ask to attend training courses. Other graduates will join companies in what they might see as a 'non-graduate job' and will seize their opportunities to progress as rapidly as possible.

So it is hardly surprising that one of the top skills sought by employers of graduates is flexibility. This is closely followed by several others that are common to nearly all employers, regardless of their line of business. The top ten skills identified by recruiters of graduates (in alphabetical rather than descending order) are:

★ Adaptability
★ Commercial awareness
★ Communication, both verbal and written
★ Initiative
★ Leadership
★ Numeracy
★ Persuasive skill

★ Problem-solving ability
★ Self-reliance
★ Teamwork.

You could add willingness to learn, commitment, ability to cope under pressure, desire to achieve and reliability, but most of these are subheadings of the above.

What do they mean in the world of work?

Adaptability

Jobs change. New working methods are introduced. Organisations' aims and objectives change. A few years on you could be doing very different work. Almost certainly you will have to attend short courses or make sure in other ways that you constantly update the skills you need to do the current job. (This is known as continuing professional development, and is a requirement in some professions.) You might need to acquire new skills to deal with the way in which the job is changing.

So much for the employers' point of view. For your own sake, you might need to re-train, change employer – or even career. The days of spending all your working life with one company are long gone. Now it is acceptable, even seen as desirable for career development, to move to different employers. You might be made redundant. The job scene at the moment certainly isn't secure!

Commercial awareness

If businesses don't make profits they go bust. OK, you are not interested in selling your soul to industry: you want to do something socially useful. Public sector organisations and charities have tight budgets to meet. Organisations are always looking for ways to reduce their costs, even if they don't have to make a profit. You'll need to understand the implications of this and appreciate why the apparently perfect solution just isn't possible. In many jobs you will also have to understand the importance of the customer/client/patient – who of course is always right!

Communication

At work you will have to not only communicate with colleagues but possibly with customers and suppliers. You might soon have to supervise or manage junior staff. You will almost certainly have to produce written reports. You might have to explain things to people who do not share your level of knowledge.

Then there will be meetings. Many people find these difficult. It's hard to know when to speak and when to stay silent. You will have had training in discussion groups as a student. Rachael Connelly, a prison psychologist (see page 70), attends a lot of these – and is expected to express her views. Being able to communicate with individuals is equally important in some jobs. Both Rachael and arrest referral worker Gail Foster (see page 95) have to draw out people who are reluctant to talk.

Initiative

Most employers don't want graduates who follow instructions, keep their heads down and keep the current system running smoothly. They want innovators with ideas, who will challenge the status quo and improve on it. 'Orange is a young, vibrant company brimming with ideas. It looks for ideas-based people, people who are excited by a culture that encourages creativity.' 'Procter & Gamble uses calculated risk as a means to accelerate change and achieve significant commercial advantage.' (Taken from the companies' recruitment material.) See also Self-reliance, below.

Leadership

This doesn't just apply to the armed forces! Managers lead. Leadership isn't about merely implementing a strategy by telling people what to do. They may need to be convinced, persuaded, helped to do what you expect of them.

Numeracy

Most jobs involve some numbers. There is a big difference, though, between understanding and feeling comfortable with figures, graphs and charts (numeracy) and being competent in calculus, geometry and algebra (maths). Luckily, as already mentioned, you should leave your social science course a pretty numerate person.

Persuasive skill

You'll certainly need this if you go into any kind of sales or promotional work. But what about meetings, again? Persuading clients or colleagues to do it your way sometimes calls for considerable powers of persuasion.

Problem-solving ability

Unless you go into research you won't just have academic arguments to weigh up. At work, you will be frustrated by budget problems, lack of time or lack of resources. Your ideal solution simply might not work. Often there is no obvious answer. You might have to compromise.

Self-reliance

Graduates are expected to work without constant supervision. This does not mean that you will be expected to be an instant expert in your job. Managing your own learning means knowing when to ask for help.

Teamwork

This means working with and for other people and getting the best out of the situation. Why 'with and for'? Because some organisations deliberately form small teams to work together on specific projects – and appoint leaders. Someone who has led one team might find that he or she is an ordinary team member on the next one.

The sad thing is that not all employers are convinced that graduates possess these skills. The Chartered Management Institute and the London College of Printing carried out a survey of 2,250 managers in 2002. Seventy-five per cent considered that new graduates had good IT skills but only 30 per cent were impressed by their ability to communicate! Sixty-four per cent were not impressed by interpersonal skills. Half of them said that graduates lacked interpersonal skills – and were not diplomatic when dealing with either colleagues or customers. Team working was rated by 25 per cent of managers and even problem-solving ability drew praise from only 20 per cent. Oh dear!

Some employers' viewpoints

Dominique Eisinger is a graduate recruitment officer with Linklaters, a City law firm that advises the world's leading companies, financial institutions and governments on their most challenging transactions and assignments. The firm recruits around 125 graduates each year to become trainee solicitors and receives several thousand applications.

Dominique says, 'About one third of our trainee solicitor intake have non-law degrees. We are interested in such students because they bring diversity to our graduate intake – not only of background but also mindset and approach. However, we apply the same selection criteria to *all* students, whether they have studied law or not – and because of our reputation and the consequent number of applicants we can afford to be picky. First we go for a good academic track record. They must be in line for at least a 2:1 and the track record must be consistent. I look right back to GCSE grades, then A-levels and marks throughout the degree course. Sometimes students say, "First year work isn't important so I didn't work very hard." That does not demonstrate consistency!'

So, what is she looking for in an applicant? 'We need people who can work in a team. I look for evidence on the application form that they have taken part in team activities such as sports, orchestra, Duke of Edinburgh, Young Enterprise and so on, rather than solitary ones like jogging or reading. They need not have been head boy or girl at school or team captains, however – just good at working with others. That said, we do also want people who can take responsibility or a lead when necessary.'

Dominique does not discriminate against students who have not had time to take part in many extracurricular activities, though. 'We realise that some students have to spend most of their free time in part-time jobs to support themselves. Team working skills can also be gained this way – but students don't always appreciate this or tell us about the skills they have developed. Sometimes they say at interview, "I didn't mention my bar job because it is very low level work. I didn't think it was important", yet the skills they can learn are real. Waiting on tables or working behind a bar gives experience of working with other people – not to mention resilience and consistency. We deem all work experience to be good work experience.'

Other qualities Linklaters look for are determination and imagination. 'We want people who will be able to find innovative ways of solving our clients' problems, perhaps in a situation where someone else would say, "That can't be done." This is hard to test on application forms', says Dominique, but could be demonstrated by the way the students have answered open questions on the application form or by creative thinking that was required to solve some problem on a gap year, for example, or in many other situations.

Commercial judgement is also important – again difficult to assess but not impossible. 'Our staff act not just as legal advisers to clients but also as business advisers. They must understand their needs. We want people who are genuinely interested in what is happening in the commercial world, rather than attracted to the City because it is exciting – and financially rewarding. They are likely to be already reading the financial press, interested in how a business works and learning about mergers and takeovers. Last, of course, we want to know what has inspired a non-law student to choose law as a profession and why they have chosen to apply to us.'

Elizabeth Selby, Graduate Marketing Officer with Masterfoods, a part of Mars Incorporated, says, 'We employ graduates as it has been proved that they have the calibre for senior managers of the future. They offer fresh ideas to the business that have not been formed into a predetermined mind state. They offer various skills and every individual is different. The two most important skills for us are verbal and numerical, but having said that we have a very open approach and our past recruits have a varied skills base. The things we try to bring out of the graduates during our recruitment process are their individual style and qualities.'

Elizabeth finds that weaknesses common to most applicants are experience and the ability to relate issues to questions during interviews. As far as CV enhancement is concerned, she says, 'We all know the student debt is in increasing, so I think work experience becomes more difficult as money is the underlying factor. I would say the extracurricular activities would be more important. Membership of any student societies such as AIESEC (a society for students interested in business careers) demonstrates that they are motivated. Also, participation in sports is a good demonstration of team work and motivation.'

And in brief:

★ 'Nestlé is looking for passion, commitment, creativity, motivation and the confidence to challenge thinking and take calculated risks.'
★ 'L'Oréal seeks graduates who can combine innovation with creativity, entrepreneurial spirit and effective interpersonal skills.'
★ 'Lloyds TSB Group is looking for people who can easily adapt to change and uncertainty; people with excellent interpersonal skills who take pleasure in getting things done with drive, energy and the ability to think laterally.'
★ 'Tesco looks for graduates with a unique blend of people, leadership and analytical skills. They need a passion for the industry and an ability to rise to the challenge of working in the exciting world of retail. Able to make decisions quickly, graduates should be flexible in their approach and comfortable with the demanding, ever-changing but ultimately supportive environment.'

All the above quotes are taken from companies' 2003 recruitment material.

How can you acquire any missing skills?

By getting involved in the whole higher education experience, that's how. You can pick up relevant transferable skills on your course, to an extent. But higher education is not simply about getting a degree. It is about developing as a person. Employers want rounded individuals. All those clubs and societies you will be able to join and all those readily available and relatively cheap sports and leisure are not just for fun. They can positively add to your CV! (Did you ever think that you would be positively encouraged to spend time on social activities at university?)

If you can develop a wide range of interests while a student, you will show potential employers that you can manage your time. Here you are with a good class of degree and yet you also spent hours a week on the sports field, doing voluntary work, not to mention propping up the Union bar. And you probably held down a part-time job as well. So, not someone who is going to faint when asked to handle several problems at the same time or meet a tight deadline.

Better still, make one of your interests a major one – and take an active part in organising.

Adaptability

Any evidence that you like new environments, travel, have worked or lived in different places, will be an advantage. Maybe you are thinking of attending a university some distance from home? Or taking a gap year – also away from home, possibly overseas? Here will be proof that you can stand on your own feet and relate to people from different backgrounds.

Commercial awareness

Even that boring job that you do already – or almost certainly will do as a student – to keep body and soul together, comes in useful here. Make notes while you are at work. You might, for instance, see examples of poor service. You might have the chance to improve them. When you are asked at a job interview what you know about commerce, you can draw on the list.

Communication

Don't stay silent in discussion groups. Take every opportunity to give presentations. Yes, you will be nervous the first few times, but it will get better. You could also get a job in a shop, bar or telephone call centre, all luckily now typical student jobs, where talking to people is essential.

Initiative

Can you make things happen? Have you organised an event? Raised funds? Started a club? Been responsible for implementing any change – perhaps negotiated a change to the course? Many universities have a student representative on departmental committees (sometimes elected, often a volunteer). As a departmental rep you could identify student concerns and speak on their behalf.

Leadership

You might see yourself as a team member rather than leader, but don't be afraid to take the lead when you get the opportunity. Employers want people who could become managers.

Numeracy

You will use statistics on your course, but a little extra always helps. Keep your mental arithmetic sharp. You might eventually have to take a numerical aptitude test as part of a company's selection process. You could, for instance, get a job in a busy bar taking drinks orders. You could also enquire whether your careers service offers the possibility to sit a practice numeracy test.

Persuasive skill

Can you get friends to do what you want? Convince them that your choice of film is a good one? When you are a student you might have to cajole your flatmates into doing their fair share of the shopping and housework. (Small things but not insignificant.)

Problem-solving ability

Application forms for jobs have a nasty habit of containing questions like, 'Describe a major achievement that you are proud of', 'Describe how you have overcome a difficult situation' or, 'Use this space to describe a problem or difficulty you have overcome and how'. Problem solving does not occur only in academic work. It's not a bad idea to keep a list of such instances, at work or in sports teams, the choir, clubs and so on in readiness for the dreaded questions.

Self-reliance

What about doing something really independent in the vacations? This could be learning a new skill, taking a job away from home, doing some independent travel – not on an organised holiday but a journey that you plan yourself.

Teamwork

Employers prefer people who participate in activities rather than spend all their time in the library. Yes they do! Collect evidence of membership of sports teams, committees, voluntary work projects, societies, choirs, a group that went on a field trip ...

You'll have noticed that some of the suggestions above make use of part-time jobs and joining in activities. There are lots of non-academic things you can do while a student that will make you more employable. You are almost certain to have a part-time job, either during term or in the vacations. You can learn a lot from even the most deadly work that could be used to impress at an eventual interview. (Working with people from different backgrounds, customer service, IT, observing how a business is run, etc, etc.) Colin Wood (see page 42) found out just how tedious – and physically hard – some people's permanent jobs are. This is a useful understanding for any future manager.

Clubs and societies

These are run by students for students and apart from the fact that joining some can help you to make friends and have a good time, they can also help you to get all sorts of skills. You could work in a team, perhaps captain a sports team, run a campaign, recruit new members (persuasion), become treasurer (numeracy), secretary (organising ability), or even chairman (leadership).

Voluntary work

You can join all sorts of organisations (and they will be crying out for help) in your university town. There will be some on campus too – like Nightline, which trains student volunteers to provide a confidential listening and advice service overnight. Joanne Briggs (see page 28) found that she developed several skills while doing charity work at university.

Work experience

A period of work experience looks good on a CV, and will certainly add to your employability. Rob Wadsworth (see page 46) realised during his second year that some relevant work experience would enhance his CV, and set about finding some on his own initiative. There are some really good schemes that provide work experience, such as the Shell STEP Programme, which places students in suitable companies. You could ask your careers service about this and about companies that provide *internships* that can be done in the vacations. Barry Griffiths (see page 54) did several with the organisation he was desperate to join – and this worked! Another organisation that can help is the National Council for Work Experience. Students can search its database for lists of jobs (see Chapter 8).

To sum up: 'To take advantage of the developing labour market, graduates in the 21st century will need to have good grades, work experience and initiative' (Mike Hill of the Higher Education Careers Service Unit).

3   Economics

What is economics?

Economics is a subject that analyses the supply of and demand for goods and services. Under this broad definition economists study issues like resources, wealth creation, distribution of wealth, inflation and unemployment.

Economics is not a course in management. If you are looking for a course that will give you a background in business, how companies are run, and in management techniques you will be better off looking under business or management studies.

Entry requirements

Although many students have A-level economics, it is not always essential, since not all schools and colleges are able to offer this subject. Entry to most courses is possible with almost any combination of A-levels. Some courses, though, require maths A-level. Most of these are BSc courses classed as science subjects. For a BSc or BA course classed as a social science, it is not a normal requirement, although you will need a good grade GCSE pass. Several universities offer both types of economics degree, so it is a question of locating the right one in the prospectus.

The content of an economics degree course

There are 1,913 economics courses, all in universities. It may be studied as a single subject or in a joint course with one or more others. Common joint courses are economics with one of economic history, philosophy and social history.

The first year of a single subject course will usually contain mainly compulsory or core modules, to ensure that every student, whatever their background in economics, has a grounding in the same topics. As you progress through the course the number of modules you may choose will become larger, and you will be able to choose them to reflect your particular interests. Compulsory modules usually include:

★ computing
★ economic analysis
★ macroeconomics
★ microeconomics
★ quantitative methods (statistics and mathematical methods).

Optional modules vary from university to university. Common ones are:

★ business economics
★ comparative economic systems
★ econometrics
★ economic forecasting
★ economics of development
★ history of economic thought
★ international monetary issues
★ labour economics
★ monetary theory
★ public economics.

So, what can you do with an economics degree?

A small number of careers use the subject directly. As a professional economist you could hope to work for the government, which is the largest employer of economists (see the case study of Joanne Briggs, page 28, for more information), financial institutions, industrial companies and international organisations. Economists advise all of these organisations on the economic implications of policy, supply and demand and on resources planning. For work as a professional economist, a higher degree is often required.

Related careers

Knowledge of economics and training in economic methods are extremely useful in several financial careers such as accountancy, actuarial work, banking (domestic, commercial and investment), credit analysis, fund management and insurance. The training that economics students receive in research methodology and analysis can also lead to work in management consultancy, market or social research and taxation work.

Other careers

For information on careers open to graduates in any discipline, see Chapter 2.

As an economist you will have an edge over some graduates in other subjects since your course will include statistics and quantitative methods. You will therefore be numerate, not afraid of handling charts and graphs and data, and can therefore also consider careers in computer programming, information technology, plus statistics and company secretarial work.

Skills gained by economics students

All the careers outlined above – and the list is not exhaustive – are open to you because your particular skills will include:

★ analysing and solving problems
★ communication
★ numeracy
★ research methodology
★ statistical techniques
★ using IT.

More detail

An annual survey of graduate destinations is carried out by the Association of Graduate Careers Advisory Services for publication in a booklet, *What do graduates do?* In this publication detailed information is given for four social science subjects: economics, geography, politics and sociology. Of the economics graduates who responded to a survey in 2001, the first year for which data are available, 13 per cent were studying full-time for a higher degree.

In *What do graduates do?*, careers entered are grouped under occupational headings, with examples of specific jobs and employers being quoted in some of them. It shows that the largest number – almost a quarter – were in business and financial work as chartered accountants, business analysts, other types of accountant and as professional economists. The next largest group were in commercial, industrial and public sector management, very closely followed by 'other secretarial and clerical occupations' (including an IT support officer in a bank), and 'business and financial associate professional work', a category which includes investment analysts, insurance managers and a research assistant at the Bank of England. Less obvious occupations included a political researcher at the Scottish Parliament, an administrator with a satellite television company and officers in the armed forces.

The Higher Education Statistics Agency (HESA) provides detailed analysis of careers entered by graduates in different subjects, from data supplied by universities and colleges. The figures for 2001, the latest year for which information is available, show that, of the 1,939 people surveyed:

★ 463 were working as business and finance professionals
★ 300 were in administrative and clerical occupations
★ 144 were specialist managers
★ 114 were managers and administrators 'not elsewhere classified'

- ★ 68 were managers in financial institutions and the civil service
- ★ 62 were sales assistants
- ★ 41 were managers in service industries.

Only job categories entered by large numbers of economics graduates are included. Smaller numbers were working in teaching, computing and catering operations.

All figures should be treated with caution. 'First destination' surveys are bound to include some graduates who are in temporary jobs to gain experience or to earn a living while making applications for 'graduate level' jobs. If asked their whereabouts just after graduating, Claire Paczko (see page 85) would have given her job title as 'court clerk' and Danny Thompson (page 39) would have given his as 'technician', whereas both used those jobs as stepping stones to satisfying careers. Also, some of the graduates in the catering category of employment were working as travel reps and chalet hosts, presumably having a year off before settling down to permanent employment.

Joanne Briggs
Assistant Economist, Scottish Executive

A-levels: Economics, Physics, Maths, General Studies
Degree: Economics (2:1), University of St Andrews

Joanne works in the Enterprise and Lifelong Learning Department of the Scottish Executive in Glasgow, where she has found a job in which she can use her degree subject directly and which contains a lot of variety.

'Economists working on the Enterprise side', she explains, 'are responsible for a number of different areas. Together with my line manager, an economic adviser, I cover regional policy, industrial policy – the manufacturing sector plus North Sea oil and gas, innovation, research and development and the commercialisation of university research. I provide analysis and briefings on all of those areas as required. Some requests are from ministers who, in addition to briefings often need information in order to answer parliamentary questions. I also provide information to MSPs (Members of the Scottish Parliament), colleagues in my own department, the Executive's press office and to members of the public who write in for information. I also get a number of requests from students for information for their dissertations.

'My work on regional policy is largely concerned with grant schemes. Under the Regional Selective Assistance programme firms can apply for grants to relocate in assisted areas. If one applies for a very large amount it has to undergo an economic appraisal. I look at its plans, estimates and forecasts and make an assessment of its suitability for funding. Where industrial policy is concerned I mainly prepare briefings on what is happening. For example, if a local company has announced a significant number of new jobs or large-scale redundancies, what effects will that have on the area? Some questions I might have notice of; others come by phone from the press office and need an instant response.

'Innovation and research and development are linked. We are currently looking at how well Scottish businesses are performing in respect of R&D and new products and processes, using statistics that have become available in the last few years. Commercialisation of university research is another new area. Related to this, I am analysing and producing a summary of the findings of a UK-wide survey into how universities are working with business, with reference to Scotland of course.

'My job is a mix of long-term projects and answering short-term questions very quickly, so I have to be able to prioritise. My plans to work for several hours on a project can be completely changed by an issue that crops up. It makes for a lot of variety. My work is not entirely desk-bound. I also go out to visit companies and to give presentations at meetings and conferences.'

Why did Joanne originally choose to study economics? 'Because it was my favourite subject at A-level. It was much more related to the real world than my two other subjects. I liked the

link to world events and the news. At university I had to do
another subject for two years and chose psychology. It sounds
odd but they have similarities. Both subjects study people's
behaviour and reactions, although one does it from the
emotional angle and the other from the financial. When it came
to choosing which one to continue, I could have opted for either.
I chose economics because I was still enjoying it so much. I also
thought that it might lead to better job prospects.'

Joanne began to think seriously about careers in the summer
before her final year. She knew that she wanted to work as an
economist and began to research what was available. In the
autumn term she found her careers service very helpful. They
sent her fortnightly newsletters with details of vacancies.
Joanne knew that the civil service had a generalist fast stream
but was not aware that there was also a fast stream for
economists. On advice from the careers service she decided to
apply for both. She also applied for some jobs in the private
sector, mainly in investment banks, but they had little appeal. 'I
really wanted to work in the public sector where I felt I could
make a difference – and where I would be able to see the results
of my work. When the Government Economics Service offered
me a job I took it and withdrew my application for the general
fast stream. My job does give me everything that I wanted – the
chance to use my subject and the variety. I never know what
my day is going to bring since things can change so quickly. It
has quite often happened that I have seen a news item on
morning television and thought, "I bet there will be a message
waiting for me about that." If there is, I have to change what I
had planned to do and give it immediate priority.'

Skills Joanne gained from her degree

★ The knowledge of the subject required in her job
★ Both quantitative and qualitative skills. 'Economics
   students deal with figures – and also learn to write essays'
★ Research skills
★ Analytical skills
★ Logical thought
★ A knowledge of computer packages
★ Skill in giving presentations

★ Ability to write in different styles. 'In one part of the course we had to write short, non-technical essays. This was very good training in writing reports that can be understood by non-economists.'

Skills learnt from university life in general

'I was on the committee of the Students' Association Charities campaign. I helped to organise street collections for several charities, which gave me experience in organisation, communication and teamwork. I organised coach travel for groups of students to cities all over Scotland – and sometimes I had to motivate people to get out of the coach and begin the street collections in bad weather. I put all this on my job application forms.'

Joanne's advice

'The graduate labour market is very competitive. Try to gain some work-related skills while you are a student. You must be able to put some "add-ons" on application forms for jobs.'

Career note

It is possible to join the Government Economics Service and many other employers with a first degree. For some jobs, particularly in the Bank of England and other financial institutions, a Master's degree is an advantage.

Matt Clifford
Trainee Chartered Accountant, Ernst & Young

A-levels: Economics, History, Geography
Degree: Economics (2:2), University of Birmingham

Matt's career route has been more complicated than those of some graduates in this book. First, he made a false start with his choice of degree course. Since he was interested in computing he opted for information systems at Leeds, but soon found the subject boring and left at the end of the first year.

He then found himself in the position of needing to take a year out. Work was soon found with British Gas in its emergency room, planning and directing where engineers were needed. This was a positive experience in that he learnt about the real world of work for the first time and developed related skills, but the job also made him realise that he wanted to get more qualifications. As a result, he applied to do economics and modern economic history at Birmingham, continuing in safer areas that he had studied at A-level. Matt enjoyed both subjects but felt economics was more relevant to the sort of work he would eventually look for.

Matt became interested in accountancy but knew that his degree classification would limit offers from the more prestigious companies. As a result he chose a different path and got on to the year-long management training scheme of Meyer International, the parent company of Jewsons, the builders merchants. Working as he trained, he was soon doing a wide range of managerial tasks, such as restructuring of prices when another firm was bought out, sales work, testing of products and at one point working under the marketing director. As he worked for several of the companies run by Meyer during the training (and placements being limited) he was at times based in Edinburgh, Lincoln and Gloucester. At one point he was leaving his home in Berkshire at 3.30am on Mondays for an 8am start in Lincoln. He then stayed there during the week in a small guesthouse and returned on Fridays. Despite this, Matt enjoyed the period due to the challenging and interesting work.

Things then got really interesting while Matt was working in Edinburgh and the Director of Jewsons in Scotland asked Matt to work directly under him. This was obviously a position that would look impressive on the CV and meant a lot more responsibility. While still technically a trainee, he was putting in successful redevelopment proposals and co-ordinating resulting projects, as well as overseeing management accounts. One profitably implemented idea of Matt's involved renting out part of a shop to another party.

After just over a year Matt was ready for a change. Despite working in accounts analysis he had no qualifications to show for it. Wanting to remedy this, he spoke to a recruitment agency which showed his (now significantly bolstered) CV to

Ernst & Young, one of the big four chartered accountants, and after two interviews he was offered a job. He now began training for three years and soon found himself working harder than ever. Almost immediately he was sitting exams, for which he was given paid leave. He studied all day at Ernst & Young's own college, then revised for several hours in the evening. Weekends were not sacred and meant several hours' study on both days.

'I found the process much harder than school or university and fairly exhausting. It wasn't that the work was more intellectual than degree level. The concepts were mostly simpler, but the volume was much greater, and I had to learn everything. The exam period lasted ten weeks, with five exams in areas such as finance, financial reporting, law and audits. As long as only one or two exams were failed it was possible to re-sit, but if you failed this you were out.' Happily Matt got through. He returned to college ten months later and after three months sat four more exams. Unfortunately the workload proved too much and he failed two, but after another three months and sitting all the exams again, he passed.

Back at work, Matt found himself driving widely in the South East, visiting a range of big clients, including Hewlett Packard and Mizuno. He was now specialising in audit work, checking that accounts were all present and correct. It has been quite interesting, with 'not as much number crunching as you'd think', and involving a lot of interviewing of key people to understand the business systems that the accounts represent. Matt now has one more year as a trainee before he qualifies. So far he has enjoyed the training, which he feels to be well structured.

Skills Matt gained from his degree

★ A detailed understanding of Microsoft Excel
★ A general understanding of businesses and the influencing factors on them
★ The economic history side gave an insight into the general patterns of market reactions, etc, throughout history.

Skills learnt from university life in general

Matt became a much more confident and independent person while at university.

Matt's advice

'Make sure you choose your course carefully. At the same time, make sure you enjoy your time. It will probably be the best time of your life.'

Career note

Most chartered accountants train *in practice* – which means with a firm of accountants approved to offer training by one of the Institutes of Chartered Accountants (ICA) for England and Wales, Scotland or Ireland. It is also possible to train in certain approved organisations in industry, commerce and the public sector. In England and Wales over 90 per cent of entrants are graduates. Once qualified, chartered accountants may work in practice, as most choose to do, or in one of the other sectors.

Other forms of accountancy are public sector and management accountancy. Graduates in any discipline can enter any form of accountancy and train in employment for qualifications of the ICA, Association of Chartered Certified Accountants, Chartered Institute of Management Accountants or Chartered Institute of Public Finance Accountancy.

Geography 4

What is geography?

Geography encompasses a range of social issues and environmental problems, from the global (for example the globalisation of the economy; possibility of climate change) to the local (for example agricultural pollution; individual spatial decision making) and spans the environmental and social sciences.

It is a subject that can be studied as an arts, social science or science degree. For this reason there is an enormous number of courses, and many universities and colleges offer at least two of the three types. There are 2,380 courses listed by UCAS and nearly all universities and colleges in the UCAS system offer the subject in some form. However, nearly half of these are in physical geography. If you are reading this book because you are interested in the social sciences it is unlikely that you will want to do this as a single subject. If you look for human geography, which is more likely to interest you, the number comes down to 266. Look only at single subject degree courses and the number reduces still further. You might also be interested in courses that do not force you to specialise and that cover both human and physical.

Entry requirements

Although students usually have an A-level in geography or a related subject such as geology or environmental science, some universities do not insist on this.

The content of a geography degree course

You may not have to specialise too early. Even though you apply for a course in human geography you may find that there is a common first year covering both that and physical geography with modules also in economic and social geography. Whether your eventual degree is a BA, BSc or even BSc (Econ) will depend on the modules you have chosen.

Core modules in human geography usually include:

★ regional, national and world geography
★ social and natural environments
★ IT skills
★ quantitative methods
★ qualitative methods
★ economic geography
★ social and political geography
★ research skills
★ field and laboratory work

with options chosen from:

★ particular countries and regions, for example Russia, North America
★ historical geography
★ social issues
★ urban planning
★ rural society
★ economic development
★ nature conservation
★ geographical information systems (GIS)
★ remote sensing – and many more.

So, what can you do with a geography degree?

You will gain some subject-specific knowledge that will be useful in a number of careers. Geography graduates who want to make direct use of their subject in a job usually first consider areas like town, urban and regional planning, landscape architecture, cartography, transport and logistics, GIS management and general practice surveying.

You will also gain so many transferable skills from studying geography that you will be equipped to enter many other careers. Geography is such a wide-ranging degree that you will gain a variety of skills. What are they? You will have spent time reading and sifting masses of material in order to write essays and give presentations. You will have done original research through fieldwork – and done so in a group, which will have taught you all about team work. Some of your fieldwork and surveys will probably have involved interviewing members of the public, so you will have skills in working with people. You will also be competent in:

★ retrieving information
★ handling data
★ qualitative and quantitative techniques.

Varying combinations of these skills will make you welcome in such different careers as finance, the civil service, local government, estate agency, estate management, the leisure industry, tourism and travel, production management, IT, computer programming and librarianship. Some geography graduates also become market or social researchers. Other organisations that employ them include public utilities, the communication industries, welfare organisations, the National Health Service and public utilities. Rob Wadsworth (see page 46) remembers that his very first lecture at university began with the lecturer saying, 'Good morning, everyone. You have come here to study geography but 25 per cent of you will leave in three years' time to become accountants'!

So, like all social science graduates you will find open to you a certain number of careers that are directly related to your subject, some that make particular use of the skills and knowledge that you will have gained on it, and a third group that will use the general and transferable skills common to students in arts, humanities and social science subjects. For information on jobs for graduates in any discipline, see Chapter 2.

More detail

What do graduates do? shows that of the geography graduates who responded to a survey in 2001, just over 18 per cent were studying full time for a higher degree or professional qualification. Of those who entered employment the largest number were working in administrative jobs. The next largest group were managers in the commercial, industrial and public sectors. Specific examples include retailing and purchasing. There were no other significantly large groups, perhaps proving that geographers enter a particularly wide range of careers. They were employed in marketing, sales and advertising, business and finance (including recruitment consultancy, personnel work, tax consultancy, charity projects organisation), surveying and the armed forces.

The Higher Education Statistics Agency (HESA) figures refer to graduates who had not studied geography purely as a physical science and show that, of the 1,131 people surveyed:

★ 110 were clerks 'not elsewhere classified'
★ 98 were managers and administrators 'not elsewhere classified'
★ 81 were working as specialist managers
★ 56 were numerical clerks and cashiers
★ 46 were working as business and finance associate professionals
★ 43 were administrative, clerical officers and assistants in the civil service and local government
★ 40 were in associate professional and technical occupations
★ 40 were managers in service industries
★ 29 went into teaching
★ 22 were managers in financial institutions and the civil service

★ 21 were working/training as architects, town planners and surveyors.

Only figures from categories containing large numbers of graduates are included. Smaller numbers became managers in transport organisations, computer programmers, sales managers, buyers and brokers.

All figures should be treated with caution. 'First destination' surveys are bound to include some graduates who are in temporary jobs to gain experience or to earn a living while making applications for 'graduate level' jobs. If asked their whereabouts just after graduating, Claire Paczko (see page 85) would have given her job title as 'court clerk' and Danny Thompson (below) would have given his as 'technician', whereas both used those jobs as stepping stones to satisfying careers.

Danny Thompson
GIS Development Officer, Royal Borough of Windsor and Maidenhead

A-levels: Geography, English Language, Biology, AS Chemistry for Biology
Degree: Geography BSc (2:1), Leicester University

Danny chose geography for his degree course because it was his strongest A-level subject and the one that interested him the most. He did not have any firm career plans before university; these developed during his course. He was surprised to find out how many options he had. 'Geography is such a wide-ranging degree that it can lead in many directions. You can cover IT, statistics, social issues, economic geography, the environment, meteorology, plus modules taken from both chemistry and biology. You can also enter careers that have nothing directly to do with geography. Three of my friends are now accountants. The course at Leicester has a combined first year in human and physical geography. In years two and three you can choose from a range of modules and become as specialised as you like, or keep your options wide open.'

Danny found that he had particular interests in cartography and geographic information systems (GIS) and from the second year onwards took as many modules as possible from these areas. It then seemed logical to look for a job in a GIS-related subject when he graduated. He succeeded in finding one, as a GIS technician with his present employer. Just over six months later he was promoted and is now a GIS development officer responsible for implementing, managing and developing a flexible GIS infrastructure to support the authority in delivering its goals. He also supervises three members of staff.

'GIS enables users to allocate data to geographical areas thereby providing a facility to check on characteristics of any given place or to see which areas meet certain criteria. There are over 100 GIS users in the borough including local government departments like Planning and Environment, Engineering, Land Charges, Highways, Waste Management, the Berkshire Joint Strategic Planning Unit and some external ones such as the police. They all use GIS in different ways to meet their own requirements. We provide support to them and also undertake specialist projects such as the Berkshire Urban Housing Potential Study.

'The police, for example, might want to undertake crime mapping. It is possible to analyse patterns of vandalism, car theft, and mugging – plot them on a map and see where the hotspots for this type of crime are in the borough. We might identify an alleyway, for instance, where groups of youths gather and cause a public nuisance. The police can make the decision to block it off or patrol more regularly. We can produce maps of any part of the borough and show on it such activity as break-ins, traffic offences or drug abuse, or we can produce ones to assist with matters like traffic control. Planning make particular use of GIS for flood control; Engineering use it for road layout and for mapping all the gas, electricity and water facilities. Planning is an obvious department to use GIS but even a department like Social Services can use GIS to help them allocate staff and resources to areas of particular need. GIS is even used in assessing Council Tax payable on different properties.

'Education is another big user. They do a lot of monitoring of distances from pupils' homes to school in deciding whether or not they can have free travel passes. We can do complex analysis of routes, taking into account distance, safety (ie, how many busy roads they would have to cross if walking) and present these facts to the officers who do the assessment. Soon after I started here I had to attend a meeting because one of my analyses was being challenged. I had to defend it in front of my own manager, the Head of Transport, plus representatives from the school and the parents. I still remember feeling a little too much in the spotlight and that my facts were being challenged unfairly. I was confident that they were correct, so I wasn't nervous. The facts passed the scrutiny of the inquiry and the child was refused the free travel pass, and Transportation saved valuable time and resources.

'My job now involves project management, user support, GIS application development both internally and externally, and constant liaison with the GIS community as a whole rather than simply doing analysis all the time, although I do take on some of the more complex projects myself. When a request comes in I decide which one of the team should take it on. I'm also helping develop a new Internet information system based on information already owned by the council, which will include social indicators such as areas of deprivation, provision or lack of facilities such as schools, libraries, shops and so on and will be available to people outside the council.

'It's a great job but project management does involve juggling several balls at the same time.'

Skills Danny gained on his degree course

★ Technical skills and techniques relating to GIS that were later developed in the training/hands-on learning he received from his employer
★ IT skills in general and familiarity with a whole range of applications
★ Time management skills and the ability to manage and present large quantities of technical data
★ Communication skills.

Danny's advice

'Don't worry too much about eventual careers if you choose geography as a degree. However, courses differ, so do look carefully to see which ones offer interesting modules. In your second year start to think a bit about what you enjoy most, whether it might lead to a job – and then take the appropriate modules to push that goal forward.'

Career note

Nearly all universities offer geography. Be careful to choose a course that offers the balance you want – towards human geography or physical geography.

You may have to take a full-time or postgraduate course in order to enter some careers.

Colin Wood
Project Surveyor, Gardiner & Theobald

A-levels: Biology, English Literature, General Studies, Geography
Degree: Geography (2:1), University of Greenwich

Colin is a chartered quantity surveyor who works for a large London-based international project cost and management company.

Like many other people featured in this book, Colin chose his degree subject for pure enjoyment. Geography had been his favourite subject since GCSE. A discussion with a careers adviser at school had not resulted in any firm career decisions but he was pleased to know that the adviser thought geography a useful subject that would keep many career options open. Although he had no particular career plans, some branch of surveying was at the back of his mind and he had done his school work experience placement with a surveyor.

At the end of his second year he began to think seriously about careers, started by researching into surveying and decided on quantity surveying. He soon realised that he would have to do a postgraduate course and consequently wrote to a number of employers listed in the Royal Institution of Chartered Surveyors' (RICS) Directory, which he obtained from his university's careers service, enquiring about sponsorship.

'I was very lucky – around at exactly the right time. Together with other large quantity surveying practices, Gardiner & Theobald had just developed a new training scheme in conjunction with Reading University. I was accepted and began the programme, under which I learnt the nuts and bolts of the profession at work and attended the university under block release for a RICS-accredited MSc in construction cost management. The course taught me a lot about management techniques and gave me an appreciation of the construction industry that supplemented the practical training I was receiving from colleagues. The RICS training is highly structured and very thorough. Every three months I had a review with a qualified surveyor within the firm who was supervising my training and signed off different competencies as I achieved them.

'The popular image of a quantity surveyor is of someone who counts bricks and argues about cost. It's far, far more complicated than that for large firms! Taking measurements may be out-sourced. Our job is to manage the cost of construction from first inception to completion. We get involved right at the beginning, at the design stage. We meet with the client, the architect and engineers and put together an estimate for the design by using our knowledge of market conditions. Clients know how much they want to spend and have some ideas on design; architects have their own ideas. Our job is to manage the aspirations of the architect within the constraints of the client's budget and the practicalities of the engineer's requirements. There is a lot of discussion at this stage – "What if…?" or, "Suppose we do it this way?" Quantity surveyors are not the most popular people on a project! It's a profession that calls for a great deal of negotiating ability. Clients always think they are paying too much, architects want to spend more and contractors think they are being squeezed.

43

'Once agreement on the design and the construction budget has been reached, our next task is to put out tenders to contractors for the construction work and for supplies. This stage can involve some travel. For example, I have been to The Netherlands to discuss a purchase of glass cladding for the building envelope. When all the tenders are returned, we will assess each bid and make a recommendation to the client. Once the decision is made to go ahead, we will prepare the contract documents and agree the contract sum with the contractor (which is hopefully less than the budget).

'An important task is to manage the budget during construction, as the nature of construction means there may be a lot of change to the original design – we have to manage this change and prepare a forecast final cost for the client at regular intervals. Naturally everyone involved needs to make a profit, but we have to ensure that costs don't spiral out of control. During the project we do monthly valuations of the work in progress so that the building contractor can be paid regularly (and pay their staff). We will also negotiate the final cost of the project. This is where disputes can arise – more need for diplomacy and negotiation!

'My company handles very large projects, for example a large headquarters for Merrill Lynch near St Paul's and the Swiss Re Tower (a new landmark building also in London). I am currently working on the Spinning Fields development in Manchester, which is a 22-acre urban regeneration project. There will be public squares, buildings – including a new head office for the Royal Bank of Scotland – and open spaces. The land has been purchased by a private property developer, but the city council has a say in the development, especially over the open spaces. It's extremely interesting and very varied work. I spend part of my week at my desk in London and part on site or in meetings in Manchester.'

Skills Colin gained on his first degree course

★ Communication skills through writing essays, a dissertation and giving presentations
★ Teamwork, through fieldwork

★ Ability to work with new people. Some fieldwork involved interviewing members of the public for surveys
★ Report writing skills
★ IT skills (spreadsheets are used a great deal in Colin's work).

Skills gained from vacation work

'I had some boring and horrible jobs, working shifts in factories and loading lorries for a distribution company. They taught me what hard work was all about and how to work with different people. In my job I could be at a meeting with clients in pinstripe suits one day and wearing a hard hat *and* talking to builders on the next.

'I also worked as a lifeguard and learnt to react quickly – and to resolve some disputes.'

Colin's advice

'You are going to spend three years or more on a degree course, so choose something that you will enjoy. Otherwise you might drop out. I have a friend who nearly did that. He didn't enjoy his course at all and although he did stick it out he found it very hard going.'

Career note

Anyone whose first degree is not accredited by the RICS (in surveying or related subjects such as planning) must take a full- or part-time postgraduate conversion course. They then normally complete a minimum of two years approved on-the-job training during which they keep a diary and logbook of their experience. At the end of this period they make a formal presentation to and are interviewed by a panel from the RICS. The programme that Colin undertook allowed him to do this while he was completing the MSc rather than having to wait until he had obtained it.

Rob Wadsworth
Regeneration Officer, Nottingham City Council

A-levels: Geography, English, History, Politics, Sociology
Degree: Geography (2:1), University of Leicester

Rob, who is a team leader in Nottingham City Council's Regeneration Division, found his job through a combination of knowledge gained on his course and work experience while doing it. 'This is a very difficult career path to embark on', he says, 'and as my degree was academic I saw the need to balance it with some practice. Whilst at university, I undertook some work experience that included working up a town centre redevelopment project and presenting my ideas both verbally and in report form. That, plus a summer job I had as an employment adviser at a Job Centre, balanced my academic degree and gave some practical skills.

'I work in the area of social economy, finding innovative ways to create jobs and reduce poverty by combining the commercial merits of the private sector and the social responsibility of the voluntary sector into a different form of company, a social company. These are companies or charities that trade like normal companies but deliver services in disadvantaged communities and are willing to train and employ the long-term unemployed. The companies are owned by local people instead of a board of shareholders. We give them business support, show them how to do their accounts and make sure they learn about appropriate legislation.' What sort of companies? 'We have, for instance, a building company that employs unemployed people and trains them. They bid for contracts in the normal way but explain that the work may take longer than usual because of the training needs. Many of the trainees move on to jobs for other building companies. Another project involves a launderette on a deprived estate. It was needed by the community, but when shops nearby started closing down the owner couldn't keep it going. A group of local people came to us for help, took it over and developed it. In addition to being a self-service launderette it now collects and delivers laundry from housebound people and is a going concern.'

Rob manages a team of development officers who work directly with the companies while he spends a lot of time on managing the project, creating trading opportunities and covering the financial aspects of the work. He also administers an investment fund from which companies can access funds to start a project. 'I ask them to produce a business plan as they would for a bank loan – but they would never be considered by banks. We make an investment but the money remains theirs'. He has to decide whether a company qualifies for assistance. 'In Nottingham social companies must trade in goods and services. (We can get that information from their cash flow records and balance sheets.) They must also be delivering services to disadvantaged communities and must pay staff either as employees or as trainees on approved training schemes. They don't have to repay the money. The return I am asking for is that they stand on their own feet, become going concerns, train and employ the long-term unemployed and show that they are benefiting people in disadvantaged communities.'

Rob's A-levels were all chosen from the social sciences. How did he decide on geography for his degree? 'I had always enjoyed human geography, which looks at how the world works. I also wanted to do something analytical.' Rob had no career thoughts at that stage but some modules in planning and economic development during the second year of the course started him thinking. He understood that it was not an easy career to break into, and decided that some relevant work experience was going to be essential. 'I started looking in the papers to see what kinds of job were available. I wrote to lots and lots of local authorities, which all said that they had no work experience opportunities in economic development. However, Oadby and Wigston Borough Council offered to let me do a project on town centre development. I worked with a planning consultant during the Easter holidays and for one day a week afterwards. It wasn't easy to fit in but I managed it. I eventually had to present the scheme to council members.'

His first job after graduation was as an economic development officer with a small district council – a job with a lot of variety and responsibility. 'I did everything from developing tourism (in an area near Sherwood Forest) and encouraging businesses to move into the area, to working in partnership with other agencies on community strategy work. We wanted to raise people's quality of life and make them proud of their community. A lot of work went on in creating green spaces and leisure facilities. We also worked closely with the police on crime prevention. The council installed better street lighting for instance, and funded a CCTV system which the police controlled.'

Rob is now doing an MSc in urban regeneration, funded by his employer who pays the course fees and gives him one day each week to attend the course.

Skills Rob gained on his degree course

★ Academic knowledge in both economic development and planning
★ Communication skills
★ Statistical analysis
★ The ability to work on several things at once
★ Report writing skills.

Skills he gained from part-time work

Communication skills plus knowledge of employment legislation and the benefits system through his work at the Job Centre. Also, 'how large organisations like councils and government departments operate, vital for an interview!'

Rob's advice

'Spend your first year at university finding your feet and developing your interests. In the second, assess which modules you enjoy most and start asking what career options they could lead to. Then, if you want to use your degree in your job, get some paid or unpaid work experience. Graduates just don't have the right work-related skills for current employers!

'There are many opportunities for graduates in the regeneration field, but you will need to understand what type of organisation you will be working for and what your role will be. It is vital to do some research on both before embarking on a career choice and applying for jobs.'

Career note

It is possible to do full-time postgraduate courses in planning, regeneration or urban development. If graduates are successful in finding employment straight away, they can do a course part time, as Rob is doing.

5   Politics

You've chosen politics, so you are going to run the world? Or the country? It isn't very likely, frankly. There are very few careers that demand a degree in this subject or even where a degree in politics is of direct use. There are some, however, and those people who enter them would usually say that there is nothing else they would rather be doing. Many, particularly those who work for campaign groups or for political parties. often work for much lower salaries than they could obtain elsewhere too!

What is politics?

Politics is the critical analysis of political systems and ideas. Some courses are combined with government and also include the study and comparison of different systems of government and administration.

Entry requirements

It is not normally necessary to have studied the subject previously. Entry to most courses is possible with almost any combination of A-levels.

The content of a politics degree course

Fifty-six universities offer degree courses in politics. Between them they offer 1,913 courses! This is because politics may be studied as a single subject or in a joint course with one or more others. Common joint courses are politics with one of economics, law, modern history, philosophy, social policy and sociology. If you want to do a single subject course your choice will be easier as there are just 48.

The first year of a single subject course will usually contain mainly compulsory or core modules with some optional ones. As you progress through the course the number of modules you may choose becomes larger, and you can choose them to reflect your particular interests. Compulsory modules usually include:

★ political analysis
★ political theory (concepts such as democracy, dictatorship, equality, liberty)
★ study of different political systems and comparative policies
★ works of political theorists like Hobbes, Marx, Mill, Plato and Rousseau.

Optional modules are numerous and vary from institution to institution. Fairly common ones are:

★ foreign policy
★ international relations
★ local government
★ political philosophy
★ political systems of chosen countries
★ revolutions.

So, what can you do with a politics degree?

Politics graduates do have a few fairly obvious careers to consider, namely politics itself. But how many MPs are there and how often do their jobs become vacant? However, add in the number of MEPs, MSPs and Welsh Assembly Members and the figure becomes a bit larger… but they don't all by any means have degrees in politics.

So where are the other jobs? The most likely are some of those in various national and international institutions – Parliament, the civil service (especially in departments concerned with policy making or advising politicians), the European Commission and European Parliament. Some graduates become clerks in the Houses of Parliament in London. They are not civil servants but 'servants of the House' and advise elected members on parliamentary practice and procedures. Others work for the political parties as researchers, campaign managers, as constituency agents or as researchers and assistants to individual Members of Parliament, as does Catherine Bray in this chapter. Others, like Barry Griffiths, choose deliberately to work in a non-partisan capacity. There are also many managerial level and administrative jobs in local government that are of interest to politics graduates, particularly those who have taken joint degrees or options in government.

Skills gained by politics students

Researching and analysing issues are major ones. You will also learn to put forward ideas and arguments clearly, while the ability to read widely, deal with vast amounts of information and pick out the relevant points are important skills that you will learn during your time as a student. Careers that make use of these skills extensively include high level work in the civil service and local government administration, as we have seen, and also law and journalism. You will be able to organise facts logically and to condense material and write concisely – a very useful ability in many jobs that call for the preparation of written reports or for making presentations. Personnel or human resources work calls for skills in developing and implementing policies, as does work in health and social services. Some politics graduates also become social researchers (if their courses have included some training in research methodology). Other organisations employing politics graduates include public utilities, transport and communication industries, welfare organisations and charitable organisations.

Time management will be another important skill that you will gain. Politics students generally have a very light lecture programme but are expected to spend a great deal of time in researching and writing essays or papers for discussion.

So, some careers relate directly to the subject, but there are dozens of alternative careers, many of which are totally unrelated to politics. Like all social science graduates you will find open to you a certain number of careers that make particular use of the skills and knowledge that you will have gained, and others that will use the general and transferable skills common to students in arts, humanities and social science subjects. For information on jobs for graduates in any discipline, see Chapter 2.

More detail

The publication *What do graduates do?* does not cover politics as a separate subject. However, some sample figures taken from a survey of 1,312 students by the Higher Education Statistics Agency (HESA) show that politics graduates were working as follows:

★ 276 were managers (in the public and private sectors)
★ 216 were doing clerical or administrative work
★ 125 were in business and finance
★ 65 were literary, artistic and sports professionals
★ 62 were in legal work
★ 56 were doing social welfare work
★ 50 were in teaching.

The figures relate to 2001, the latest year for which information is available. Only the largest categories are included. Others were catering operations, service industries, sales, security and protective services, librarianship and transport.

All figures should be treated with caution. 'First destination' surveys are bound to include some graduates who are in temporary jobs to gain experience or to earn a living while making applications for 'graduate level' jobs. If asked their whereabouts just after graduating, Claire Paczko (see page 85) would have given her job title as 'court clerk' and Danny

Thompson (page 39) would have given his as 'technician', whereas both used those jobs as stepping stones to satisfying careers.

Barry Griffiths
E-Democracy Programme Assistant, Hansard Society

A-levels: Politics, Sociology, History
Degree: Politics (2:2), Leicester University

Barry chose politics for his degree course because it was his best A-level subject and the one that interested him the most. He was not a member of any political party, nor particularly interested in party politics. What did interest him were current affairs. He therefore chose a degree course that was broad based, with options that would allow him to specialise as his other interests developed. He also took care to choose universities where a dissertation was not obligatory, since he preferred exams.

Barry found the entire course interesting, and to his surprise he developed some interest in studying different political parties. 'I grew up in the period of successive Conservative governments. That was all I knew until the 1997 election when New Labour got in.' He also enjoyed studying South Africa – 'We had some brilliant lectures on apartheid' – US and Russian politics and the ideologies of different political theorists.

What pointed Barry in the direction of his future career, however, was his discovery of the Hansard Society during his first year. He had become particularly interested in democracy and the democratic process. Having found out about the Society and its campaigns, he did an unpaid internship (work experience placement) there during the summer vacation. 'After that they couldn't get rid of me! I pestered them constantly for information and was there every vacation.'

The Hansard Society, which was formed in 1944, is an organisation that tries to promote effective parliamentary democracy. It is an independent, non-partisan educational charity, whose president is the Speaker of the House of Commons and vice-presidents are leaders of the three main political parties. Its aims are to provide a neutral public space in which those with an interest in Parliament can come together to study and debate; to generate opportunities for people to find out about Parliament and how it works; and to provide a forum for informed discussion about the future of parliamentary democracy. Among other things its staff conducts research and produces reports and discussion papers, often on behalf of the UK Parliament, Scottish Parliament and National Assembly for Wales combined (for example, *The Challenge for Parliament: Making Government Accountable*).

As an intern, Barry was 'a general gofer. I answered phones, did filing, helped out wherever I could. I tried to find out as much as possible very quickly, making myself indispensable – and I was soon given things to do on my own initiative. One was to organise the Chairman's retirement party at the Tate Modern. I sent out all the invitations including ones to every MP, selected Peers and dignitaries – and got a buzz out of seeing "RSVP Barry Griffiths" at the bottom.'

Barry went back to the Hansard Society on graduating, and two months later was taken on permanently. In his job he works in a small team and provides support to his programme director. 'There are five programmes of work within the Hansard Society, each run by a director and two or three staff. I work in the E-Democracy Programme whose remit is to use new technologies to further political engagement and participation. For example, the Parliament and Government programme is concerned with the modernisation of parliamentary government amongst other things. We added information on the website recently on *Opening up the "usual channels"*, ie, parliamentary whips, and brought into the open what they actually do. Another programme, based on the promotion of citizenship education, involves producing educational material for schools – projects such as *Y vote* and acting as the liaison between MPs, MEPs and schools in their constituencies – to enable visits from the elected representatives to the schools.

'We run a lot of online consultations. Basically, anyone can register on the website and take part in a discussion or receive regular updates on a topic. We are doing one right now at national level on the Anti Terrorism, Crime and Security Act. At a more local level we did one on rural transport problems in Suffolk. Anyone who has registered and knows about the Bill in question can post a message or viewpoint on one of the sections. We do a weekly summary and forward these to the appropriate select committee. Eventually we do a final report. It's brilliant making sure that people's views are reported like this.

'At the moment I'm working on a project called *Wired up Communities*, paid for by the Department for Education and Skills. In some rural areas where there is very little Internet use, the Department has paid for 1,000 people to be wired up. That means that we can now conduct online forums and I have set up some online meetings at set times with prearranged agendas. I'm enjoying working on this. It takes me out of the Westminster circle yet I am working on cutting edge democratic technology and tools – all about current or proposed legislation.'

Skills Barry gained on his degree course

★ Knowledge of the political process
★ Training in use of the Internet
★ Training in writing reports
★ Time-management skills.

Barry's advice

'Find out about careers that your degree can lead to, early on in your course. Contact former students if you can. My university invites me back to talk to students.

'Do some voluntary work and get involved. There are loads of small organisations, charities, etc that will be only too happy to take you! Once you have targeted a few organisations that interest you, make a quick phone call to their office to find out the name of their director or appropriate person to write a letter to asking about internships. A personal letter goes a very long way. Furthermore, think seriously about your future in the first year of university. Don't wait until it's too late! When you have found one – make yourself indispensable. You might get a full-time job out of it, or, failing that, a good reference.'

Career note

Nearly all universities offer politics. Be careful to choose a course that offers the balance you want. For example, does it contain international relations if this is likely to interest you?

If you are aiming for a career in politics try to get some experience working in a national parliament or government department. Some universities are able to organise work placements with UK or European Members of Parliament, with US congressmen, or at the European Commission; this will normally be stated in their prospectuses.

Tim Guymer
Planning Assistant, Winchester City Council

A-levels: Economics, Government and Politics, AS Levels in Accounting, Law
Degree: International Politics and Strategic Studies (2:2), University of Wales, Aberystwyth

'All my A-level subjects had been new to me. I didn't have a GCSE background in any of them. When it came to choosing a degree subject I decided to continue with one I enjoyed – but from a different angle. I had done enough government, I felt, and although I did do some of this in my first year, I was able to concentrate on international relations. The degree was a very good preparation for this job. It taught me that there is always more than one way of looking at things. There are more sides to a story than the media would often have you believe. I did my dissertation on "Was the Gulf War a just war?" for instance, and benefited from being taught by people who knew more about it than we had seen on the television news. I also learnt to analyse how twentieth century conflicts have arisen and been resolved, and also studied the role of leaders and the impact of people in power. Believe it or not, much of this translates to dealing with planning issues. It helps to see where people are coming from, what their agenda is – are they genuinely interested in the good of the community or simply their own small area? I also, of course, knew how government works.'

Tim works for Winchester City Council and is still training. Most local authorities provide very good, *free* training (which is important to a graduate!) and Winchester is no exception. Tim spends one day a week at Reading University, studying for an MSc in planning, with all his course fees paid. 'It's hard work doing it this way. I have to spend at least 15 hours a week on additional private study (and did more in my first year). It will take me three years to obtain the MSc but I much prefer doing it this way to borrowing money to fund a full-time course.' In any case the topics he studies at university back up the practical training he is receiving at work. He also enjoys meeting students from other subject backgrounds on the course since they have a variety of views on how to approach issues that arise.

Tim works in a local planning team, which means that his job changes constantly. 'Reviewing the local plan is a five-year process. We are now at the next round of consultations – taking the plan to the public and asking for opinions. Winchester City Council covers a large rural area as well as the historic city itself, so we take exhibitions to centres in villages, produce explanatory booklets and now put information on the Internet. A wider audience is likely to see the plan that way. I have been involved in passing all the key information to our IT staff. I read all the letters and comments that come in and summarise them, and get some verbal opinions as well. People often come in person to tell us what they think of the plan – and their views are not always complimentary! I have to stay cool and explain that the decisions are being taken by the people they elected to represent them.

'I enjoy the consultation side. I love meeting people and getting their views. I enjoy the policy side too. Planning is a question of balancing arguments, weighing them up and trying to find the best solution to recommend to councillors. We also have to comply with legislation from central government. Right now the number of new houses to be built in the South East is a contentious issue.'

Tim says that it was work he did in his gap year that most influenced his eventual career decision. He had planned a year working for a charity in London but this fell through, and he spent the year in a series of temporary jobs to earn money. One of these was with the NHS. It was at a time when old mental hospitals were being closed and patients transferred to smaller establishments. Tim helped to do much of the physical work involved in closing wards, but also became interested in what was to happen to the patients and to the hospitals that were listed buildings but sold for development. He also did a lot of voluntary work for his church, working with the elderly, running young people's discussion groups, doing some administrative work and being a general 'gofer'. Both experiences contributed to his thinking: 'I knew that I wanted a role in changing the way society develops but I wasn't sure about a particular job.' It was not until he was taking a second gap year, after finals and again working for the church, that he found his way into planning. He saw an advertisement for an administrative assistant in his present department, applied for it and worked there until an opportunity for a planning assistant came up.

Skills Tim gained on his degree course

★ To view a problem from all angles
★ To avoid one particular mind set
★ To balance an argument, for instance weighing up the different merits of residential properties, businesses (and consequently jobs) in a given area, taking into account the likely increase in traffic.

Skills he gained from part-time work

'Diplomacy and the ability to cope with angry people were two valuable ones. For a while I collected the fees for using a car park owned by the church. People were always arguing over how much they had to pay.'

Tim's advice

'Don't assume that your degree will lead you into one job only, or be an automatic guarantee that you will get a good job. But don't panic. You will gain a wide understanding of issues and a lot of skills that can be transferred to the work place.'

Career note

Local planning is the responsibility of local government. Elected councillors actually control planning decisions, but planning officers and assistants produce policies and advise councillors on strategic and operational aspects of planning.

Graduates usually take either a two-year full-time course approved by the Royal Town Planning Institute, or a three-year part-time one as Tim is doing. It is also possible to qualify through distance learning while in employment, or to take a first degree in planning.

Catherine Bray
Political Adviser, European Parliament

A-levels: English, History, Politics
Degree: Politics (2:1), University of Leicester

Catherine found her job, as so often happens, partly by being in the right place at the right time and partly through relevant work experience. In her case it was the *offer* of doing voluntary work that gave her her first break! She intended to take a gap year to earn some money to finance a MA course, but spend the summer doing voluntary political work. As soon as finals were over she went to her local Conservative Party office and asked if there was any voluntary work she could do there. By sheer good fortune the wife of one of the region's MEPs (Member of the European Parliament) was visiting the office. She told Catherine that her husband had a vacancy for someone to do a three-month stage (paid work experience placement) and suggested she contact him. Catherine did the placement, and at the end of it found a permanent job with Christopher Beazley, the Conservative MEP for the Eastern Region.

Her job has many strands. 'First there is basic administration. I answer the phone, feed information into the computer, reply to letters – we receive ten to 15 each week from constituents in the UK – and write newsletters for the UK constituency to make sure that people know what is happening. We work very closely too with the MPs in the area and make sure that they are fully briefed on current issues. We often refer matters to each other since some people write to us and others write to their local MP with questions or comments on Europe. Every other month I go back to Hertfordshire and talk to Party agents to find out whether they have what they need or require any more information. We also arrange visits from time to time for people from the constituency to come to Brussels and meet relevant people. For example, the EU constitution is going to be amended. Some people are unhappy that there will be no reference to religion in it. We recently arranged for the Bishop of St Albans to come to Brussels and put his point of view to MEPs on the committee dealing with the constitution.

'On the political side I follow events both in the UK and in the rest of the EU. I read a lot of reports and summarise them. If there is something that specifically affects the UK, MEPs can put down amendments. I also keep in touch with group meetings of the Centre Right, which UK Conservative MEPs are aligned with. I had to go to a meeting yesterday since Christopher had to be in the UK. I can't take part in meetings but I can attend and take notes. Simultaneous interpretation is provided through headphones. Each MEP is a member of certain committees. Christopher is on the one dealing with culture, education, media and sport, known for short as the Education Committee. I have to keep up with everything that committee does and read all the minutes.

'One week in four the Parliament moves to Strasbourg. That is a really, really busy time. All MEPs must attend plenary sessions and vote on the final stages of legislation. Debates often go on until midnight. I make sure in advance that Christopher knows if particular reports will be coming up and that he has them to read. I can see the debates, which are televised, from my office and see the votes. I record all the votes and do some political analysis of how UK MEPs have voted on sensitive ones. It's useful for us to know how opposition MEPs have voted!

'A big issue right now is the enlargement of the EU. A lot of people want to know how it will affect them. Recently we organised a conference in Hertfordshire for local business people. A colleague and I got high profile speakers from Lithuania, Latvia and Poland to speak to them and explain how their prospects could improve through the new trading opportunities. I did everything – found the speakers, booked the venue, sent the invitations and wrote press releases for the local papers.

'I meet so many interesting people in this job and no two days are ever the same.'

Catherine chose to do politics because it was far and away her best subject at A-level. She liked everything on the course, found political philosophy particularly useful 'as a basis that helped all the other modules', and enjoyed the freedom of the final year when she could concentrate on her favourite – South African politics. Had she not found the job at the European Parliament, she would have done an MA on that aspect. 'I will one day. After a few more years here I should have saved enough to do the course. Eventually I want to teach politics.'

Skills Catherine gained on her degree course

★ A grounding in European politics, policy and institutions (compulsory modules)
★ Communication skills
★ Report writing skills
★ To manage her time and to prioritise.

She had to do two subsidiary subjects in the first year and chose economics and sociology, reluctantly. 'I just wanted to do politics – nothing else. At the time I didn't realise how I was learning to keep on top of several different things. Now I have to balance committee, Group and constituency work as well as dealing with anything else as it arises.'

Skills she gained from part-time work

'I learnt to deal with difficult customers when I worked in a supermarket coffee shop. I use that skill now since I often have to take angry phone calls.'

Catherine's advice

'Do your homework when you are filling in your UCAS form. However hard you work, you won't do well if you don't enjoy the course. I chose one with lots of options. I also chose one that offered final year exams *or* fewer final year exams plus a dissertation. Most people did the dissertation but I chose exams because I work best under pressure.'

Career note

It is possible to do stages for individual MEPs and also at the EU Commission. To find out more, contact your MEP or the Commission office in London (see Chapter 8).

It is not necessary to speak French. Most business is conducted in English or through the interpreting services available. Language lessons are offered for staff wishing to take them.

6 Psychology

What is psychology?

Psychology is the scientific study of human and animal behaviour, how people (and sometimes animals) behave, react and interact. Psychologists use scientific methods to collect information about normal and abnormal behaviour. The information gained is used to understand behaviour and, by practising psychologists, often to modify it.

Entry requirements

Some degree courses have a more biological bias than others, are regarded more as a science than a social science subject, and are likely to require an A-level in a scientific subject. Entry to most courses, however, is possible with almost any combination of A-levels.

The content of a psychology degree course

There are 119 institutions (mainly universities with some colleges of higher education) that offer degree courses in psychology. It may be studied as a single subject or in a joint course with one or more others. Some single subject courses are known as cognitive behaviour or behavioural science. There are specialist courses in applied consumer psychology, clinical psychology, developmental psychology, health psychology, neuropsychology and organisational psychology.

A single subject course in general psychology will usually begin by giving students a good foundation and grounding in the subject. It is not necessary to have done the subject to A-level, although many students have done so as it is now more widely taught in schools.

How do you choose one?

First of all it is important to know whether you might want to become a professional psychologist. If you do, it is advisable to pick one that is accredited by the British Psychological Society (BPS). In order to become a chartered psychologist and practise the profession you must follow a BPS-recognised postgraduate training. (In fact anyone may call himself or herself a psychologist but reputable employers know that qualified psychologists have their names on the BPS register of chartered psychologists.) The easiest route to training for chartered status is to have a first degree that the Society also recognises. Without one, you can still train, but it will take longer and involve conversion courses. Most university and college prospectuses state whether their courses are accredited. If not, or if you want to be doubly sure, you can check with the BPS direct (see Chapter 8). There are 2,074 degree courses with the word 'psychology' in the title – so it's definitely worth checking!

Psychology courses contain compulsory or core modules that usually include:

★ cognition
★ developmental psychology
★ human development
★ individual differences
★ perception and learning
★ physiological basis of behaviour
★ research methods
★ social psychology
★ statistics.

Optional modules are almost limitless and vary from institution to institution. Fairly common ones are:

★ aggression
★ artificial intelligence

★ auditory perception
★ child psychology
★ clinical psychology
★ health
★ human communication
★ language acquisition
★ legal psychology
★ neuropsychology
★ occupational psychology
★ organisational cultures and change
★ personality
★ psychology of education
★ psychology of sport
★ psychopathology.

Since the choice of options varies it is important to be sure that the courses you choose contain modules that will both interest you and introduce you to any professional career in psychology that you might be considering.

So, what can you do with a psychology degree?

All psychology graduates become qualified psychologists. Right? Wrong. This is certainly an obvious career move, but if every psychology graduate hoped to enter the profession there would not be enough jobs to go round. Luckily, this is a subject that has many potential uses.

First there is the direct use of the subject in a career as a chartered psychologist. Next comes a range of related careers in which considerable use is made of the subject knowledge and skills gained on the degree course. Third, almost any career in which knowledge of human behaviour is required can be of interest to psychology graduates. Finally, there are the 'careers open to students from any discipline' category. These are outlined in Chapter 2.

Professional psychology

The British Psychological Society defines six types of professional psychology:

1. Clinical (applying psychology to people with health problems or severe learning difficulties, mainly in NHS institutions such as hospitals and clinics)
2. Counselling (alleviating stress or temporary crises or helping clients to understand their problems and develop solutions to them)
3. Educational (concerned with children's learning and development and involving much work in schools)
4. Forensic (working within the justice system, in courts, prisons, rehabilitation units and special hospitals)
5. Health (relatively new – working on provision of health care, problems of public health and response to illness)
6. Occupational (concerned with organisations, training and performance of people at work).

These are all described fully in an excellent careers booklet produced by the BPS, *Careers in Psychology, a Graduate Guide*. In addition, there are opportunities in teaching and research.

Related careers

Psychological knowledge – and often techniques – are extremely useful in several careers that involve working closely with other people. These include audiologist, careers adviser, coach/personal trainer, community worker, Connexions Service personal adviser, counsellor (not all counselling situations require a chartered psychologist), housing manager, human resources manager, occupational therapist*, police officer, prison governor, probation officer, recruitment consultant, social worker, speech and language therapist*, teacher*, lecturer, training officer, youth worker, and – any kind of management job. (* Further full-time training would be required.)

There are several careers in which knowledge and understanding of human behaviour are important, such as advertising, market research, public relations, sales and social research. In all of these, information on what influences people to buy, think, or behave in certain ways is required. For information on careers open to graduates in any discipline, see Chapter 2.

As a psychologist you have an advantage over some graduates in other subjects. Your course will include statistics. You will therefore be numerate, not afraid of handling charts and graphs and data, and so can also consider careers in computer programming, finance, information technology, plus qualitative and quantitative research.

Skills gained by psychology students

All the careers outlined above – and the list is not exhaustive – are open to you because your particular skills will include:

★ Analysing and solving problems
★ Communication
★ Conducting experiments and research
★ Numeracy
★ Using IT.

More detail

What do graduates do? shows that 11 per cent of psychology graduates were studying full time for higher degrees (including investigative psychology, cognitive and affective neuroscience, developmental psychopathology, Internet computing and human resource management). Five per cent were studying full time for a professional qualification in teaching, a figure that most probably includes many future educational psychologists who are first required to qualify as teachers and gain teaching experience before continuing professional training. Nearly 5 per cent were taking other full-time courses, for example in law, and 62.9 per cent were in employment in the UK.

The largest number were in administrative and clerical work (20.7 per cent), closely followed by professional and technical occupations including welfare, community and youth work, psychology, clinical psychology and social work (18.9 per cent). Some of these would be following part-time professional training courses on a salaried basis. Next came health and childcare professions such as mental health work, counselling, project work and child development work (14 per cent) and commercial industrial and public sector management (11.6 per cent). Smaller numbers entered marketing, sales and advertising (3.6 per cent) and teaching (3.7 per cent). Less obvious occupations included tax accountancy, insurance, banking, contracts management and scientific indexing.

The Higher Education Statistics Agency (HESA) analysis of careers entered by psychology graduates shows that, of the 794 people surveyed:

★ 145 were in social welfare and health professions
★ 103 were doing administrative and clerical work
★ 66 were working in business and finance
★ 48 were sales assistants
★ 46 were managers and administrators 'not elsewhere classified'
★ 40 were specialist managers.

Only job categories entered by large numbers of psychology graduates are included. Smaller numbers were working as, for example, managers in national and local government, large companies and service industries, and in air traffic planning and control.

All figures should be treated with caution. 'First destination' surveys are bound to include some graduates who are in temporary jobs to gain experience or to earn a living while making applications for 'graduate level' jobs. If asked their whereabouts just after graduating, Claire Paczko (see page 85) would have given her job title as 'court clerk' and Danny Thompson (page 39) would have given his as 'technician', whereas both used those jobs as stepping stones to satisfying careers.

Rachael Connelly
Forensic Psychologist, HMP Nottingham

A levels: Psychology, Business Studies, Economics, History
Degree: Psychology (2:1), University of Leicester

Rachael works as a psychologist at HMP Nottingham, a local or holding prison where convicted prisoners are sent straight from the court to be held while arrangements are made to categorise them and transfer them to training prisons where they will serve the remainder of their sentences.

Rachael chose to do psychology knowing that she wanted a career as a professional psychologist, although she was not sure at this stage which branch of the profession she would choose. She therefore took care to ensure that the courses she applied to were recognised by the British Psychological Society and would lead to the status of a chartered psychologist (see Career note for further details).

Her first degree was wide-ranging and interesting. Rachael particularly liked abnormal, child and legal psychology. She was less keen on neurological psychology and statistics. The BSc was, however, general and theoretical; it was on Rachael's MSc course that her work became more 'hands-on'. Forensic psychologists must do an accredited one-year course in forensic psychology and complete two years of post-qualifying work experience (supervised training on a salary) before they become fully qualified. Rachael stayed at Leicester to do the MSc, which included an eight-week placement at HMP Nottingham. At the end of the course she successfully applied for a post there and is now almost at the end of the training period.

Rachael's work consists of *interventions* with prisoners. These may be one-to-one sessions or group work. Her one-to-one work takes the form of meetings with individual prisoners and deals mainly with coping skills for adjustment to prison life. 'I see vulnerable men who are being bullied, some who may attempt to harm themselves, some who need to learn anger management, and also some who are suffering from earlier trauma or abuse.'

Interventions vary in different prisons, she explains. In a holding prison, prisoners are not there for long, so interventions are necessarily brief. Prisons apply for Home Office funding to run certain programmes (all accredited by the Home Office and following specified syllabuses). They might, for example, run programmes for sex offenders or prisoners convicted of violence. Nottingham and four other prisons are piloting two-week courses for short-term offenders, most of whose sentences are for 12 months or less. Rachael tutors one course each month.

'Obviously we can't change people in two weeks. But hopefully we can motivate them to think about changes that are possible and that there are areas of their life that could benefit from change. There are people who see nothing unusual in being constantly in and out of prison. We aim to challenge that. The first week consists of mornings only and is based on psychology. In the second week we work in the afternoons as well and here we cover practical topics like housing, money management, debt control and drug or alcohol dependency.' The courses are hard work and demand good group-work techniques. Rachael enjoys them and finds that most prisoners are very receptive and co-operative. 'They have all previously been interviewed, regarded as suitable, and offered the opportunity to attend. Some find discussion daunting at first but we manage the group carefully and gradually most take part.'

When she is not tutoring or conducting interventions with individuals, Rachael's time is taken up in writing reports on prisoners, including parole reports and risk assessments, or attending meetings of several prison committees, including suicide, anti-bullying and race relations.

She is almost at the end of her post-qualifying experience period, during which she has had fortnightly supervision meetings with a chartered psychologist and has had to produce a portfolio of evidence showing her competence in four key roles: conducting psychological applications and interventions; research; communicating psychological knowledge and advice to other professionals; planning and design of training.

Skills Rachael gained on her degree course

★ Theoretical knowledge of psychology, which formed a base for professional training
★ Social and communication skills
★ Skills in group work, acquired in discussion groups
★ Presentation skills
★ Report writing skills
★ Time management.

'Many of these skills are directly relevant to my work now.'

Skills gained from part-time work

'I had a series of temp jobs in secretarial and administration work. These were helpful in teaching me to work with other people and to build up relationships in a short time.'

Rachael's advice

'Try to get some experience related to the type of work you might want to do. While I was a student I was a voluntary support worker in a bail hostel run by the probation service.

'You might have to start as a psychological assistant, as I did, to gain experience before being promoted to psychologist.'

Career note

Most universities and some colleges offer courses in psychology. Not all (especially some joint courses) are recognised by the BPS. It is still possible to become a chartered psychologist from a non-recognised course, but professional training would take longer.

There are different training pathways for the different branches of psychology. As soon as you know which one might interest you, try to arrange some relevant work experience or voluntary work so that you can apply for a postgraduate course or training programme. Clinical, counselling, educational, forensic, health and occupational psychologists follow different training programmes, which last three years on average.

Darren Johnson
Personal Adviser (Careers Guidance specialism), Centre for British Teachers (CfBT), Thames Careers Guidance

A-levels: Sociology, Psychology, History
Degree: Psychology and Sociology (2:2), University of Kent

Darren enjoyed all of his A-levels but, being particularly interested in understanding people and cultures, decided on the joint degree course in social science subjects rather than one in history.

He enjoyed psychology so much that he took as many modules in it as possible, making up about two-thirds of his programme. He particularly liked the biological aspects and spent time working in mental hospitals, looking at depression, psychosis and the effect of institutionalisation, and also worked extensively with young offenders. He did not enjoy the maths and statistics involved – something he had not expected. He soon began to think about using psychology in a career.

After graduation Darren decided to take time out and found a job in a youth hostel near his home in Norwich for six months, where he also worked part-time with young offenders. Soon, however, he decided to do something totally different before settling down: he found a job as a social host on a cruise ship going around the Mexican Riviera and Caribbean Islands. He had to organise and co-ordinate social activities and do some compering of shows. He stayed for over three years.

Eventually Darren decided to finish on the cruise ship and return to England. He now had to make a career decision. He knew that for a 'serious' job more training would be required, and considered a number of options. Originally he thought about accountancy or the Foreign Office, but found that the best companies were only interested in people at most two years out of university. Darren also considered a PhD in psychology but was put off by the prospect of more debt, 'partly due to the fear that came with my working-class background'. Careers advice appealed as it was linked to his degree and his interests, and after only a year's training a job was guaranteed.

Careers advisers working with young people visit schools and colleges to give careers talks, lead group discussions and conduct interviews with individual pupils in which they discuss their interests and aptitudes and provide them with relevant information to help them in making education and career choices. They may organise careers conferences and write information material. In order to stay up to date they have to do a good deal of research and visit employers, training providers and educational establishments.

Darren has now been qualified for three years. He first worked in a community team, dealing with young people who had dropped out of education before 16, but his interests have changed and he now advises school pupils between the ages of 14 and 18. 'I changed partly because the community work is very stressful, dealing with pupils with very difficult problems, but I also feel it is important that all young people are well informed and motivated to get good qualifications.'

Darren normally spends three days a week at a local school, dealing with students in Years 9–13. He interviews eight students a day, to discover their ambitions and to explain their options. At the college he also sees higher education students on Higher National Diploma courses who range in age between 18 and 30. Several times each month he runs group work sessions with students, showing them how to use the careers library, and helping them identify their abilities and weaknesses in relation to the job market. He also arranges for visiting speakers to give vocational talks. Once a month, he visits employers to get an insight into what they are doing. Currently he is enjoying the job, but feels it has changed a lot.

Government initiatives have made careers advisory work more bureaucratic, with less time for clients than before.

Skills Darren gained from his degree

Research capability, which is useful for retrieving job information from a range of sources. During his degree he spent a lot of time interviewing young offenders and looking at why they fall into crime, as research for his dissertation. This is relevant as one of the biggest parts of his job is interviewing young people to find out their needs and thoughts on life and careers.

When Darren did his training in careers guidance he found he had covered almost all relevant areas (especially psychometric testing) in his psychology degree. Sociology has helped him to understand people of different cultures, necessary when dealing with the needs of asylum seekers – something he sometimes has to do.

Skills gained from student activities

Darren was involved competitively in football, tennis and volleyball. He was the captain of some of the teams, learnt a good deal about people, and developed organisational ability as he arranged social events for the teams. Captaining sports teams boosted his confidence and helped him develop leadership qualities.

Darren's advice

'Although any subject will qualify you for careers advice training, one that involves looking at cultures and people will be relevant. Before starting the training, see if you can shadow somebody to get a feel for it.

'And be aware that employers may not be impressed by too long a gap between university and training for a career.'

Career note

Careers advisers who work with young people as Darren does are part of a new service, Connexions, which provides advice and guidance to young people between the ages of 13 and 19 on a range of issues including health, financial and personal problems. Connexions staff are known as personal advisers. Some are careers guidance specialists, who take a one-year full-time or two-year part-time qualification in careers guidance, then are trained further by their Connexions Partnership. (Connexions Partnerships are responsible for different geographical areas.)

Careers advisers in universities have a variety of backgrounds. Many have worked in industry and commerce, while others have worked for Connexions Partnerships or their forerunners, local careers services.

Kate Gillan
Trainee Clinical Psychologist, Greater Glasgow Primary Care NHS Trust

Highers: Biology, English
Degree: Social Sciences (2:1), Queen Margaret University College, Edinburgh

Like two other people in this book, Kate did not go straight to university on leaving school. Having obtained what she describes as 'not too spectacular qualifications', she followed her interest in health care by training to be a registered general nurse. Then, 'I had done a psychiatry block as part of my nursing training and found mental health interesting. I also became aware of the need for psychological support for those who were experiencing physical problems. I decided that I wanted something that would allow me to apply psychological theory and research skills to physical and mental illness, and so applied for the psychology-based degree course. (Although the title is social sciences I took the health psychology option.) I felt that psychology would lead to a career in that field, although at that point I knew very little about the work of a clinical psychologist.'

Kate discovered more about the work when she did some relevant modules in her final year, and found that she enjoyed them. A lecturer suggested that she consider clinical psychology. Kate thought about it, looked into the length of time needed to qualify – and was relieved to discover that she would be paid throughout the training period.

She is now in her second year as a trainee. 'It was actually quite stressful getting this far. For clinical psychology, it's not just a question of applying for higher degree courses immediately after graduation. It's extremely competitive. I spent 18 months in a psychology assistant post before getting this position, a three-year doctorate with Glasgow University. I am sure that my nursing experience helped with my application.'

As a psychology assistant Kate observed the work of several qualified psychologists and was allowed to do some work with patients, but always under tight supervision. 'For example, I could be asked to do some anxiety management with an individual or a group of patients who had already been assessed by a psychologist. I would do so under the psychologist's guidance. I also did things like relaxation work with burns patients and ran some anxiety management groups jointly with an occupational therapist. I was lucky to work in St John's Hospital on the outskirts of Edinburgh. It is a community and acute hospital treating all kinds of patients and has specialities like child, family and adult psychiatry, plastic surgery and a major burns unit. It also has a large psychology department. So I got a good range of experience. I also did some research during the period I spent there.

'I am now based in the Department of Psychological Medicine at Glasgow's Gartnavel Hospital where I have my own caseload and am given referrals. I work under a supervisor who observes my casework and in turn allows me to observe her. Sometimes this is done by tape or video, but always with the patient's consent. I am given cases that offer a taste of a wide range of aspects of psychology, and placements are arranged for me in outpatients' departments and in other hospitals to gain experience in certain areas. I have done a placement in learning disabilities, for example, which meant staying midweek in Dumfries, and I will soon be doing a child placement in another area.'

What can I do with... a social sciences degree?

What sort of casework does Kate do? 'In adult mental health I have worked with patients with eating disorders, addictions, brain injury, anxiety and depression. Anxiety disorders and clinical depression are some of the most common referrals. With someone who is depressed I will perhaps spend the first two sessions making an assessment. I will look at predisposing factors such as any early experiences that have perhaps resulted in the person becoming vulnerable to depression. And what is maintaining the depression? Following assessment I can begin to formulate treatment. The majority of my training is cognitive behavioural in origin. I may begin to work on the behavioural side, gradually trying to take the patient back to things they used to enjoy by activity scheduling. I might ask them to keep a diary and note things they have enjoyed doing recently. The cognitive aspects involve identifying a person's thought patterns. If someone thinks that they are a failure, where have these negative thoughts come from? I'll encourage the patient to challenge these beliefs by asking them to provide counter-evidence for their negative thoughts. It doesn't work every time, of course. Some patients simply don't like introspection; some may want a different approach to treatment. For example, cognitive behavioural work involves lots of homework exercises to encourage the patient to use the techniques outwith the sessions.

'I love the work. It is immensely satisfying. I am dealing with people who are distressed but begin to feel for the first time that they can be helped. Every patient has a different story to tell. They have different personalities, lifestyles and have had different upbringings. Some have seen horrendous things or witnessed horrific violence. I develop a close relationship with my patients and we talk about things that have become entrenched in their lives. It can be stressful. I cannot afford to let any problems I might have at any time affect my work and I have to meet the academic deadlines for my doctorate.

'I am a doctoral student at the same time as being a salaried employee. Last year in term time I spent two days at the university, two at the hospital and had one study day. This year it's one day at the university, three on placement and the one study day. In the university vacations I spend three to four days on placement. I have to take my annual leave then too. I am not allowed to take days off in term time.

(Training patterns vary in different regions. I know for instance that in Edinburgh trainee clinical psychologists spend blocks of time at the university.) In order to qualify I have to conduct a research project and write it up as ready to be submitted for publication. I also have exams to pass, case studies to write based on my clinical work, and will have to discuss a portfolio of cases with examiners.'

Skills Kate gained on her first degree course

★ Theory, which she draws on heavily in her job
★ Skill in researching and writing essays
★ Communication skills
★ Ability to meet deadlines
★ Ability to juggle several different tasks.

Skills she gained from previous employment

'Nursing taught me skills in working with patients.'

Kate's advice

'Do a degree that has BPS accreditation. It takes a long time to catch up otherwise.

'Get some relevant experience. You could do part-time or vacation work while you are a student.

'Work hard! You will need a 2:1 or above.'

Career note

See under Rachael Connelly, page 70.

7 Sociology and related subjects

This is a very big subject area with various possible combinations of sociology, anthropology and criminology. There are over 2,000 courses, and you can study these subjects in almost every higher education institution. There are only 25 single subject courses in anthropology, however.

What is sociology?

Briefly, it is the study of relations between people in contemporary and historical society and relationships between different societies in the world system. The subject also looks at institutions within a single society, culture, social policy and welfare, and considers issues such as social change, social conflict, divisions between social groups, social problems such as homelessness, poverty and unemployment, plus political strategies for resolving them.

Sociology is not the study of individual behaviour. If this interests you, see Chapter 6 on psychology. Neither is it a training course for social work, although anyone who has become interested in this during the course and has chosen appropriate options will have a very good background for specialist training. There are also distinct courses in social work.

Entry requirements

Sociology is a very popular A-level and many students have already studied it before going to university. But it is not necessary to have done so, and entry to most courses is possible with almost any combination of A-levels. Most courses, though, require maths at GCSE level.

The content of a sociology or related subject degree

Sociology may be studied as a single subject or in a joint course with one or more others. Common joint courses are sociology with one of anthropology, criminology, economics, geography, politics, psychology and social policy, although it can equally well be combined with history, languages or indeed most arts and social science subjects.

The first year of a single subject course will usually contain mainly compulsory or core modules, to ensure that very student, whatever their background in sociology, has a grounding in the same topics. Compulsory modules usually include:

★ introduction to sociology
★ crime and deviance
★ education
★ gender issues
★ research methods
★ social psychology
★ sociological theory
★ the family
★ the media
★ work and leisure.

You will usually have the choice of some optional modules in the first year and many more in the second and third years as your interests develop. Optional modules vary from university to university; common ones are:

★ childhood
★ globalisation
★ globalisation and development
★ popular culture
★ racism
★ social care

★ social movements
★ social policy
★ sociology of health, illness and the body
★ sociology of organisations
★ youth and society.

You can see that this is a very broad discipline. Some of the options are similar to ones offered on human geography or politics courses.

Anthropology

What is the difference between anthropology and sociology? Very simply, the main difference is that sociologists tend to study their own and similar societies while anthropologists concentrate on other, smaller ones. But there is some overlap.

In the past anthropology was perceived as the study of exotic tribes and cultures, and it did indeed develop from attempts to understand the lives and culture of non-Western people. It *does* involve the study of human groups, but the subject has moved on and is no longer primarily concerned with apparently technologically simple societies. Today anthropology studies human societies and cultures with an emphasis on contemporary peoples. It covers all aspects of human society and sub-cultures within it – those in the third world plus different ethnic and sub-groups in America, Europe and so on.

Criminology

This is a relatively new but growing subject that examines problems of crime and responses to them from sociological and social policy perspectives. If you chose this subject you would study some topics from economics, psychology, law and ethics and would take modules like criminological theory, penality, the justice system, police and society, organised crime and violence. You would also train in research methods.

So, what can you do with a degree in sociology or a related subject?

No careers demand a degree in sociology. Unlike psychology there is no postgraduate training necessary to practise as a professional sociologist. Some careers, however, are particularly relevant and make direct use of the subject knowledge and skills of sociology. A significant number of sociology students each year decide that they would like to do some kind of work involving helping other people. Some become social workers, helping people who have problems ranging from homelessness or addictions to mental illnesses. Some work with the elderly, others with children and families. Some graduates go into probation, community or youth work. Other options include becoming a prison governor, housing manager, counsellor or welfare rights adviser.

Others use the academic skills gained on their degree courses to move in a different direction and become social researchers, carrying out research for government departments and independent research consultancies, while others use the same skills in policy making roles in local authorities or the civil service.

Skills gained by sociology students

Your particular skills will include:

★ The ability to analyse and solve problems
★ Independent judgement and critical debate
★ Communication
★ Numeracy
★ Research methodology
★ Statistical techniques
★ Use of IT.

So, the following careers will also be open to you: administration and fundraising work with charities, information management, computing and IT, librarianship, management in the NHS, human resources management and recruitment consultancy. The training that sociology students receive in research methodology and analysis can also lead to work in management consultancy, market research, insurance and financial work.

For information on the careers that will also be open to you because they do not require a degree in any specific subject, see Chapter 2.

More detail

What do graduates do? shows that of the sociology graduates who responded to a survey in 2001, just over 11 per cent were studying full-time for a higher degree or professional qualification, including social work. Of those who entered employment, the largest number were working in administrative jobs. The next largest group were in varied professional occupations, including research, recruitment consultancy and IT work. Next came those working as managers in the commercial, industrial and public sectors. Specific examples include general management, retailing, distribution and purchasing. Some went directly into social work types of job, for example as a student welfare officer, support worker with Mencap and probation officer. Unusual jobs included a fraud officer with a bank, a pensions manager, a media executive and a conference organiser.

The Higher Education Statistics Agency (HESA) figures for 2001, the latest year for which information is available, show that of 2,454 people surveyed:

★ 257 were in health and social welfare work
★ 209 were in clerical and administrative occupations
★ 185 were managers and administrators 'not elsewhere classified'
★ 136 were specialist managers

★ 103 were numerical clerks and cashiers
★ 98 were managers in service industries
★ 90 were working in business and finance
★ 78 were doing clerical and administrative work in the civil service and local government
★ 76 went into teaching
★ 48 were in security and protective service occupations
★ 46 were managers in financial institutions and the civil service.

Smaller numbers were in travel, tourism, transport, sales, computing and literary and artistic professions.

All figures should be treated with caution. 'First destination' surveys are bound to include some graduates who are in temporary jobs to gain experience or to earn a living while making applications for 'graduate level' jobs. If asked their whereabouts just after graduating, Claire Paczko (see below) would have given her job title as 'court clerk' and Danny Thompson (page 39) would have given his as 'technician', whereas both used those jobs as stepping stones to satisfying careers. Also, some of the graduates in the catering category of employment were working as travel reps and chalet hosts, presumably having a year off before settling down to permanent employment.

Claire Paczko
Legal Adviser and Researcher, Home Office Funded Project

A-levels: Sociology, English Literature and Language, Media Studies
Degree: Sociology with Criminology (2:2), University of Teesside

Claire works at My Sister's Place in Middlesbrough, part of a Home Office funded crime reduction programme: the Violence against Women initiative. My Sister's Place provides support and legal advice to women who have experienced domestic violence, and is the only one of its kind in the North East. Claire's advisory role involves the provision of initial legal information to women using the centre, and representing them in court as and when required. On the research side she also tracks cases through the court system to identify loopholes and the difficulties women can face in accessing criminal justice and civil remedies.

Claire has 233 current clients. Just two examples show the kinds of problems she deals with. One involves a professional woman with two children who had suffered violence from her husband for 15 years. Broken bones and fractures were run of the mill to her. When she suffered facial fractures and a collapsed lung she finally snapped, tried to obtain legal aid, for which she was not eligible, then went to My Sister's Place. Claire says, 'We applied for and obtained a DIY injunction. This means that the applicant applies for it in person. The problem comes if it is contested: she ends up facing her assailant in court and effectively has to cross-examine him and any other witnesses. I therefore went to court and acted for her. I felt that we had grounds for a non-molestation order under the Family Law Act – and obtained it. He turned up once, was arrested, and there have been no further incidents.'

The second concerns a young mother who suffered terrible violence. On the last occasion her husband came home drunk, accused her of wearing too much make-up, dragged her downstairs by the hair and knocked her unconscious against a radiator. When she came to he was using a hot iron on her face to try to remove her make-up. Claire says, 'The police did respond but she was afraid of him and of his friends. We obtained a court order prohibiting him from coming within 100 metres of her property, making any threats, harassment or intimidation. He did try – and came back claiming to be full of remorse. She called the police. He was arrested and eventually sent to prison.'

Claire's interest in this type of work began when she explored domestic violence as part of her degree course, which she had originally chosen because, she says, 'I wanted to examine the diversity of society and, as I had studied deviancy during A-level sociology, I was particularly interested in criminality. During the degree I learnt there was more to people than meets the eye.'

Claire's favourite modules included culture and society, which examined patriarchal cults and male dominance; criminal justice, 'which opened my eyes to policy and procedures – the evolution of the system and the pattern of work of the police and the Crown Prosecution Service'; and sociological theory, in which she studied the concept of the criminal personality, social control and asked questions like, 'Why punish?'

The domestic violence module came during her second year. Claire looked at the myths and realities, the legal responses to domestic violence, and wrote her dissertation on the judicial responses to domestic homicide. 'There is no doubt', she says, 'that I wouldn't be doing my present job if not for that course. We looked at the dynamics of domestic violence and some of the myths, such as the false claim that it's a working-class problem. Studies show that violent men come from every economic or social background.'

After she graduated Claire took some time out and worked as a rep for a company organising holidays for 18–30 year-olds. Based in a busy resort in Cyprus, she learnt to cope with situations ranging from over-exuberant behaviour by young people on holiday without their parents for the first time, to helping a client who had lost all his possessions when on a short cruise to Israel. 'I did it to have some fun before I got onto the career ladder, but I learnt a lot of useful skills in dealing with people in just one season!'

She then went on to gain a postgraduate diploma in law, the essential first step for training to be a barrister or solicitor. To generate some income, she worked as a court clerk for various solicitors in the North East. The main aim of these jobs was to pay the bills, but like the Cyprus job they gave Claire valuable experience, this time in court and advocacy work. She now took some time to consider her next step. Becoming a barrister, she decided, would involve too much financial commitment. She had already taken out a career development loan to finance the diploma course and funds were running out. She was offered a training contract with a firm of solicitors, which would have enabled her to qualify as a solicitor while still earning some income from court clerk work. As she was about to accept she saw her present job advertised, 'spent a long Christmas agonising', and decided to apply for the post with the project.

Claire admits to being an idealist. 'I'd love to change the world! However, as that's not possible I can sleep well at night if I have helped just one person during the day. And I might come back to the idea of being a barrister later on. Nothing is impossible.'

Skills Claire gained on her degree course

★ Objectivity
★ Essay-writing skills, which can be transferred to report writing
★ To argue and present a case. 'I'm preparing a funding bid at the moment, which calls on all the skills I used in doing my dissertation'
★ 'I developed an enquiring mind and learnt how to ask the right questions'
★ 'I learnt to re-examine things I had previously taken for granted. You shouldn't judge a book by its cover. There is so much more to life.'

Skills gained from her temporary job

★ To think on her feet
★ To work long hours, 'sometimes it was as though I was on call 24 hours a day'
★ To relate to and communicate with a wide range of people.

Claire's advice

'Don't panic about being boxed in if you do a social sciences degree. It won't restrict you in any way. It's a very valuable qualification to have. You can't study social sciences without learning all about people. I would say it is an essential subject for any profession that involves dealing with people.'

Career note

Several universities offer courses in criminology, as a single subject or in combined courses.

Claire obviously uses her legal knowledge and experience, but has not found it necessary to qualify as a solicitor or barrister in order to do her job. If you did wish to train for either profession, you would first have to take a conversion course in law (one year full time or two years part time) followed by a further professional course (again, one year full time or two years part time). You would then do a period of professional training in chambers to become a barrister, or with a firm of solicitors in order to become a solicitor.

Sonja Wellings
Policy and Research Officer, Harvest Housing Group

Access to Higher Education Course
Degrees: Sociology (2:1), University of Salford
MA (Econ) Applied Social Research, University of Manchester

Sonja did not go to university straight from school. Higher education was not in her thinking then; instead she went to work and had a series of office jobs. It was when she was made redundant that she took a close look at where she was going and decided that she wanted to do more with her life. So she enrolled on an access to higher education course, specialising in political history and psychology.

> 'I actually applied for a degree course in psychology but did not get the grades I needed. So I went into Clearing and found that I could be accepted for sociology, at Salford near where I live. I didn't want to leave the area and therefore accepted the place. I enjoyed most of the course, particularly the theoretical subjects like sociology of technology, towards post-modernity, ethnographic texts and visual representation. I was less interested in topics like criminology, crime and society, and identity and kinship. The syllabus was very broad however, and I was able to tailor the course towards my interest by choosing appropriate modules.'

Sonja started to think seriously about careers at the beginning of her final year. She found out that she had a very wide career choice but, 'I didn't want a job using my degree as a general

89

qualification. I wanted to use my subject.' Research was her main interest and she realised that she would need a specialised higher degree in order to enter a competitive field. There was no course that seemed quite right in her own department, but Manchester University offered just the one she wanted. Sonja enrolled on a two-year part-time course and continued to work in part-time jobs to pay her way.

Again, she tailored her degree very carefully. 'I could have done some straight sociology modules on the MA but I deliberately chose to concentrate on qualitative and quantitative research, methodological issues and data analysis.' Her department's policy was to assign research projects to students where possible, and Sonja was soon asked to undertake one on behalf of the Harvest Housing Group. That led to her present job.

'I was offered permanent employment as soon as I had my MA. Harvest Housing is a housing association that owns 15,000 properties in the North West. The association rents properties similar to those owned by local authorities in their social housing stock. In other words, most of the tenants are in need of low cost rented accommodation. Anyone may apply but those with the greatest need are housed first. Seventy per cent of our tenants are either unemployed or on benefit. There are 80 members of staff in the Manchester office. My department is called Strategy and Information. There are just two of us – myself and a research assistant.

'My job has three parts. One is research. I design and conduct my own research projects. Another is policy. This means that I have to review our policy to see whether it complies with government policy. My third role consists of monitoring our performance. My work is very project-based. I always have several in progress at the same time, and they cover a range of different areas. I have conducted a major tenant satisfaction survey, for example. For this I commissioned an outside agency to visit people and ask the questions, but I managed the project. I also work very closely with other agencies. For instance, I have done some work on a project to evaluate spending of budgets allocated under the government's Single Regeneration Budget initiative for inner city areas. My part has been concerned with investigating housing sustainability in deprived areas, looking into factors like de-industrialisation, population migration and resulting demand for housing. There is a lot of secondary socio-economic data to analyse when looking at what happens in small areas.

'My day varies according to the projects I am engaged on. I spend some time on background reading of policy documents, write reports, plan and design questionnaires for surveys, or analyse secondary data, often using the Internet. I am currently analysing figures from the last census and applying them to our area. I do some of my work at home because I work in an open plan office and it is not always possible to concentrate.

'I enjoy what I do in my job but what I also appreciate is the amount of independence I have. It's up to me to prioritise, to decide what to concentrate on and to organise my work. This is exactly what I had to do on my degree courses.'

Skills Sonja gained on her first degree course

★ To research and write essays, which translate into report writing skills
★ Communication skills
★ To manage her time and to prioritise
★ Analytical ability.

Skills gained from the MA

More of the above – 'but more in depth and with more training in critical thinking and in managing my time and working independently. I gained all the skills I needed to walk into this job and start work. I am the only researcher in the office. There was no one here to show me what to do. I was taken on as a fully qualified member of staff.'

Skills gained from part-time work

'I did bar work throughout both my courses and learnt to deal with people. I also worked in a call centre, where I certainly gained communication skills.'

Sonja's advice

'To study sociology you must be interested in reading widely and writing essays. The subject gives you a good grounding in many subjects, but is not a vocational course. I wouldn't have been recruited to this job without a Master's degree.'

Career note

Most universities and several colleges offer courses in sociology. It is possible to enter some kind of social or market research work from this degree. Some forms of policy or specialist research work will be easier to enter if you taken quantitative and research methodology options on the course. Some jobs like Sonja's, where graduates are not recruited as trainees but as experienced workers, will require further study.

Philip Robinson
Development Worker, Housing Project for Single Parents

Access to Higher Education Course
Degree: Youth Studies (2:1), University of Teesside

Philip was one of the first students to graduate from his degree course, one that combines several subjects including criminology, psychology and sociology.

Philip, from Redcar, left school at 16 and originally aimed for a career in the Royal Marines. Circumstances forced him to change his mind, and he gained a post as a sales assistant in an independent clothes shop. Following this, he trained as a carpet fitter, working in the trade for two years before going back to retailing.

By the time he was 22 he realised that he was 'going nowhere' and began to study psychology at evening classes. He later decided that university was for him and enrolled on an Access course at Redcar and Cleveland College. He knew at this point that he would like some kind of career connected with young people, and this course seemed just right. 'I always felt I'd be suited for youth work. I'm interested in excluded youth and related issues. When I began the Access course I was aiming for a Diploma in Social Work, but then I saw a leaflet about the new Youth Studies degree and thought, "That's what I want to do." It seemed to me to be much broader and could lead on to careers in social work, youth work, the probation and Connexions services or work in hostels, and other jobs I probably didn't know about.'

The course was wide-ranging. Philip particularly enjoyed psychology related to young people, and criminology, which examined the criminal justice system and the way the courts work. He also found the historical overview interesting. 'We studied the changes in youth culture during this century plus the media's perceptions of young people now as compared to in the 1940s. We also looked at young people's views of drugs, which I explored in my final year dissertation. For the dissertation I interviewed a random sample of six people aged 18 to 29, looking at their views about the normalisation of recreational drugs, such as cannabis and Ecstasy. The results were interesting. The majority didn't want Ecstasy de-criminalised, for instance, because of the health implications.'

When he graduated Philip had no firm career plans. Then he saw a post advertised for a development worker with Coatham House, Redcar, a National Lottery funded project for teenage mothers. He applied for it and got it. It's a new job, which gives him plenty of responsibility and scope to develop the post. 'I'm employed to develop a project for single teenage parents. (Although most will be women, it is always possible that we might have a male client, so I changed the name from the original "Single mothers".) For the project to assist them, they must be homeless or being threatened with homelessness – in other words their families might throw them out. The project will soon have three two-bedroom houses in which one parent can live with their baby. The idea is that they stay for one year, with support, learn how to live independently, cook, budget, manage utilities bills and so on, then move on and get their own homes.

'I'll do initial assessments and work out what support the clients need, how much I can provide, and when we will need to call on other professionals. I have spent time developing links in the community and so will be able to refer them to social workers, health visitors, counsellors, people who can help with benefit claims and also to Sure Start, a support group for single parents with children under 5.

'I have been responsible for purchasing and furnishing the houses. Originally we hoped to buy four, but with the way house prices are shooting up, it has come down to three. I did all the house hunting and spent time looking for properties in a central area close to amenities, so all the local estate agents got to know me well! They are all nicely decorated and furnished and include cots and baby equipment. Two are now ready to be occupied and the third will be soon.'

Skills Philip gained on his degree course

★ 'The degree certainly helped me to get this job. Certain modules explored issues around teenage mothers; I now have a lot of knowledge in this area'
★ Social and communication skills
★ Report writing skills: 'very useful since in the initial phase of the project I had to write a policy and document all the procedures we would be following.'

Skills gained from voluntary work during his course

'I worked as a volunteer with the probation service and with the Youth Justice Courts. I gained more knowledge and understanding of the age group and I acquired counselling skills.'

Philip's advice

'If you have a specific career area in mind, do research your choice of course properly. I went through the entire UCAS handbook looking for courses in youth work or in social work with relevant options. I had found some and made a shortlist – then saw the publicity for the new course, which just happened to be at my nearest university.'

Career note

Several universities offer courses in youth and community work, youth and community development and similar titles.

It is obviously possible to get a related job straight from university, as Philip did. Other options include taking a Diploma in Social Work (DipSW), which may be done on a full-time basis or through part-time courses and distance learning while in employment, or becoming a probation officer. The only way to qualify for this work is to gain employment as a trainee probation officer and follow a planned programme leading to the award of the Diploma in Probation Studies. (In Scotland probation officers hold the DipSW.)

Gail Foster
Arrest Referral Worker, NHS Funded Project

A-levels: Business Studies, French, English Literature
Degree: Criminology (2:1), University of Teesside

Gail had no idea about a future career when she applied to university. She chose her course, therefore, for no other reason than to do something interesting and decided on criminology because it offered a variety of subjects. 'There was so much to choose from that you could tailor the degree to your own interests. Although I didn't know then that I would eventually work with drug addicts, I was particularly interested in society's growing drugs problem. When I was comparing criminology courses I saw that Teesside offered modules in the subject.

'So I particularly enjoyed a module, "Drugs, Crime and Society", where we asked how people become addicted and examined the typical "career path" of a criminal. As part of another module we visited a local prison and while there we looked at their drug strategies. I also enjoyed a study of youth perspectives, where we explored how young people grow up, progress through life, the choices they make and how things can go wrong.'

Gail wrote her dissertation on the government's ten-year drug strategy, and is sure that the detailed knowledge of drugs that she gained through doing her research was the deciding factor in gaining her present job, which she began soon after graduating. 'I was young and had no training or experience, but the interview panel could see that I had a sound knowledge of different drugs and their effects. I wasn't starting from scratch.'

In her job she advises drug addicts held in police cells on appropriate treatment services, health, and harm minimisation. She can also advise on housing if the clients have no fixed abode. Posts like hers are funded differently across the country; in her case the NHS provides the funding. In some areas it is done by charities.

Gail is based at Middlesbrough police station where she works a shift pattern of 7.30 to 15.30 or 1.30 to 21.30. 'When I come on duty I go first to the custody suite and ask if anyone who is being held there wishes to see me. If not, I usually go to the cells, explain who I am and that I can offer advice. If they then accept, we move to an interview room. I spend between 45 and 60 minutes with a client. I first try to establish the reason for their addiction. It might be due to the death of someone they love or to social circumstances. I might be able to offer positive help by arranging bereavement counselling or literacy classes. Of course I try to encourage people to go for treatment and if they agree I write down some details and arrange an appointment for them at the appropriate agency. (I had to spend some time when I first started visiting different agencies, introducing myself and building up relationships.) If they say "No" to that, I can at least warn them about the risks of hepatitis and HIV and offer advice on safe injection.

> 'I can't provide answers but I can listen, sympathise and advise. It is important to me to speak to my clients as human beings. They may not have received much respect before. I don't always know whether I have had any impact but I do follow up my clients. I try to find out when their court dates are so that I know whether they have been discharged, placed on remand or sent to prison – and whether I can refer them to appropriate people. I also ring the agencies where I have made appointments for people, to ask whether they attended.

I get a buzz when I find out that someone who I didn't think would go has actually thought it over and done so.

'The arrest referral scheme had been running in Cleveland for a couple of years before I joined, so the police had already got used to us. Police officers have always been very friendly and co-operative towards me. However, when the scheme began I think they were quite sceptical.'

Skills Gail gained on her degree course

★ A knowledge base where drugs are concerned
★ Understanding of the criminal justice system and workings of the legal system.

Gail's advice

'It's difficult to advise anyone how to get into my job. If you want to be a police officer, social worker or probation officer, the training route is all mapped out. For me it was a case of answering a job advertisement I saw on the NHS website and hoping to prove that I had the right skills.

'If you want to get into this or any other kind of social work, try to get some work experience. There are plenty of opportunities for voluntary work. I wish that I had done some. I spent some of my spare time as a student working in paid jobs to support myself. That was important, but some relevant experience would have been helpful too.'

'Before you choose a degree course look carefully at different ones and see what options are offered. Courses with the same title are not identical. For me, choosing one with the chance to specialise in drugs was important.'

Career note

Several universities offer courses in criminology, as a single subject or in combined courses.

What can I do with... a social sciences degree?

It is obviously possible to get a related job straight from university, as Gail did. However, see her advice above. An alternative route would be to take a degree course in social work.

Sources of further information

8

Books and booklets

Careers in Psychology, A Graduate Guide, produced by the British Psychological Society (see below).

Graduate Career Directory, Hobsons. Annual publication giving details of employers and their vacancies. Also contains careers information in the form of job descriptions.

Graduate Salaries and Vacancies, Association of Graduate Recruiters (AGR)

How to Succeed at Assessment Centres, Trotman

Prospects Directory, AGCAS. Annual publication containing details of employers and their vacancies. See also website

Skills for Graduates in the 21st Century, AGR. Can be consulted on their website

The Trotman Careers Directory. Contains descriptions of over 300 careers

What can I do with... a law degree?, Trotman

What can I do with... an arts degree?, Trotman

What do graduates do?, CSU in association with UCAS. Can also be found on the *Prospects* website

Websites

Association of Graduate Careers Advisory Services: www.agcas.org.uk

Association of Graduate Recruiters: www.agr.org.uk

British Psychological Society: www.bps.org.uk

The National Council for Work Experience: www.work-experience.org

Prospects Web, a higher education careers website: www.prospects.ac.uk/student/cidd, contains many useful career profiles, and www.prospects.ac.uk/workbank, for work experience options

University of London Careers Advisory Service:
www.careers.lon.ac.uk, for *How to analyse and present your skills for work*

Addresses

British Psychological Society
St Andrews House
48 Princess Road
Leicester LE1 7DR
Tel: 0116 254 9568

European Commission Information Office
8 Storey's Gate
London SW1P 3AT
Tel 020 7973 1992

Government Economic Service
Economist Group Management Unit, HM Treasury
Parliament Street
London SW1P 3AG
Tel: 020 7270 4835
Website: www.ges.gov.uk

Society of Business Economists
11 Baytree Walk
Watford WD17 4RX
Tel: 01923 237287
Website: www.sbe.co.uk

UCAS Distribution
PO Box 130
Cheltenham
Gloucestershire GL52 3ZF
Tel: 01242 544610